The Noise of Solemn Assemblies

The Noise of Solemn Assemblies

CHRISTIAN COMMITMENT AND THE RELIGIOUS ESTABLISHMENT IN AMERICA

BY

Peter L. Berger

GARDEN CITY, N.Y.
Doubleday & Company, Inc.

Grateful acknowledgment is made to the following for permission to reproduce extracts from copyright material in this book:

American Council on Education: from "The American Tradition and the Relation Between Religion and Education" in *Religion and Public Education*.

Association Press: from *How to Serve God in a Marxist Land* by Karl Barth and Johannes Hamel.

Beacon Press: from *Protestant and Catholic* by Kenneth Underwood.

Constable & Co. Ltd.: from *Middletown* and *Middletown in Transition* by Robert S. Lynd and Helen Merrell Lynd.

Doubleday & Company, Inc.: from *The German Phoenix* by Franklin H. Littell. Copyright © 1960 by Franklin H. Littell.

The Free Press of Glencoe, Illinois: from *The Passing of Traditional Society* by Daniel Lerner.

Victor Gollancz Ltd.: from *Brighter than a Thousand Suns* by Robert Jungk.

Harcourt, Brace & World, Inc.: from *Middletown* by Robert S. Lynd and Helen Merrell Lynd, copyright 1929 by Harcourt, Brace & World, Inc.; renewed 1957 by Robert S. Lynd and Helen Merrell Lynd. And from *Middletown in Transition* by Robert S. Lynd and Helen Merrell Lynd, copyright 1937 by Harcourt, Brace & World, Inc.

Harper & Brothers: from *The Authoritarian Personality* by E. W. Adorno, and from *The New Shape of American Religion* by Martin Marty.

The Macmillan Company: from *Religion, Society and the Individual* by J. Hilton Yinger.

National Council of the Churches of Christ in the U.S.A.: from the *Revised Standard Version of the Bible*, copyrighted 1946 and 1952.

Princeton University Press: from *Small Town in Mass Society* by Arthur Vidich and Joseph Bessman. And from *The Eclipse of Community* by Maurice Stein.

Public Affairs Press: from *Christians in Racial Crisis* by Ernest Campbell and Thomas Pettigrew.

Simon & Schuster Inc.: from *The Organization Man* by William H. Whyte, Jr., copyright © 1956 by William H. Whyte, Jr.

University of North Carolina Press: from *American Protestantism and Social Issues* by Robert Miller.

The D. Van Nostrand Co. Inc.: from *What College Students Think* by R. K. Goldsen, M. Rosenberg, R. M. Williams, and E. A. Suchman. Copyright 1960, D. Van Nostrand Co. Inc., Princeton, New Jersey.

Yale University Press: from *Millhands and Preachers* by Liston Pope. And from *The Living and the Dead* by W. Lloyd Warner.

CONTENTS

I hate, I despise your feasts, and I take no delight in your solemn assemblies.

Even though you offer me your burnt offerings and cereal offerings, I will not accept them, and the peace offerings of your fatted beasts I will not look upon.

Take away from me the noise of your songs; to the melody of your harps I will not listen.

But let justice roll down like waters, and righteousness like an ever-flowing stream.

AMOS 5:21–24 (RSV)

I

Preface on Perception

While this essay addresses itself primarily to Christian students in the American situation, it might also be said to speak both out of and with reference to a more general state of mind in this country. This state of mind might be called a sort of Christian malaise, not unlike the feelings one sometimes harbors for a beloved but hopelessly impossible relative. It expresses itself again and again in the embarrassment of intelligent Christians as they speak about their churches. And the malaise is not limited to the laity. At least within the Protestant domain (which is our main concern here) it may be found with frequency in the formal and informal gatherings of clergy.

As this state of mind is met with criticism from outside, there is often a strangely ambivalent reaction compounded of a defensive rejection of the criticism and an almost masochistic relishing of its sharpest jabs. This ambivalence may be observed often among students who come from backgrounds where religion is taken for granted and who are exposed for the first time to the pressures of an intellectually alive campus. Of course, there are many whose relationship to the intellectual life remains so marginal that this taken-for-granted religiosity continues into later life virtually unscathed. There are some (probably quite a small minority) for whom this point in their lives marks a definitive and conscious break with their religious past. Others take refuge in a permanently defensive posture, a reaction all too often encouraged and nurtured by the religious organizations on the campus. Others again learn to live with ambivalence, alternating between affirmation and embarrassment, as particular social situations dictate. This last reaction may quite possibly be that of the majority.

It is a regrettable fact of our cultural situation that such capitulation to permanent half-honesty is often interpreted as a sign of "maturity." By contrast, the intellectual passions of rebellion are seen as simply a symptom of "immaturity." It may happen in such cases that the one moment in an individual's biography when questions of truth and authenticity are at least glimpsed becomes neutralized by looking upon it as just part of a process of sowing one's wild oats. The rest of life then becomes a more or less comfortable settling down with the half-truths or even the organized delusions which are embodied in the various social institutions. Both love and truth become at best the subject matter of nostalgic reminiscence.

We would argue, on the contrary, that the moments of intellectual passion, far from being phases in a process of "growing up," are the crucial points of decision in life. This is why the years in which one is a student are of such importance. With a minimal involvement in society in terms of external commitments and responsibilities, these years can be those in which the basis for an authentic existence is built. They can also be the years which fixate for the rest of life an existence of inauthenticity, dishonesty, and bad faith. This is true of an individual's religion as much as of his other involvements in the world and in society.

However, we would argue in this fashion not only from general considerations concerning the value of a life which retains the intellectual ecstasies of youth. We would argue further that the Christian faith itself forbids its being interpreted as the religious rationalization of a process of "maturation." We would maintain that Christian commitment demands a relentless intellectual honesty, because it concerns God, who is truth and who is offended if He is worshiped as anything less than truth. Finally, it would seem that in our situation there is a special call for such intellectual toughness in being willing to perceive the social reality of religion. It may well be that the decisive *skandalon* for Christian commitment in our time is precipitated not by history or biology or psychology but by sociology (meaning by this not so much these scholarly disciplines in themselves but the perspectives on religious phenomena resulting from them).

A few words of elaboration on this point may be in order. Since the writer of this essay is a sociologist, it is quite possible, of course, that this statement reflects his particular bias and experience. However, it would seem that the statement bears examination in terms of the larger background of Christian commitment in our time. It almost seems as if different disciplines succeed each other in a mission of debunking and unmasking the pretensions of religious positions that refuse to face up to the demands of intellectual integrity.

The historical study of the Bible constituted a tremendous intellectual challenge to Protestant complacency when it began to subject the sacred records of the Christian religion to scientific study. Then followed the Darwinist and Freudian challenges to what Christians took for granted as their view of the world. For people coming today from conservative Protestant backgrounds, these challenges still involve vital tests of their intellectual integrity, as the experience of many teachers can verify. Nevertheless, we would argue that, to those whose religious position is grounded in what this essay will call our religious establishment, these challenges commonly mean no more than minor shocks. Protestant theological students, let alone those in undergraduate courses in religion, manage to absorb with relative calm the news that neither the Old nor the New Testament is the inviolate record of divine truth that they thought it to be in Sunday school. Evolution is typically a religious problem only to the less sophisticated groups. And as to the challenge of psychoanalysis, an age in which bus drivers own up to "rationalizations" and office girls work hard on their "repressions" is hardly one that is going to blink too much when one points to sexual symbols in the vocabulary of religion.

On the other hand, it has been the writer's repeated experience that the same sophisticates will respond with furious resentment when attention is directed to the sociological functions of religion. If nothing else, this fact points to the erosion of genuine religious contents that has taken place. It is only natural that this should happen when religion rarely implies a specific view of the world and of history, let alone a specific inner experience of the individual. Where religion is mainly a matter of social establishment, a part of the taken-for-granted order of society, it is understandable that the debunking effects of sociological analysis bring about the severest shocks. This point will hopefully become clearer in the course of this essay. For the moment, let it stand as a preliminary explanation of why the passionate will to truth is of paramount urgency in the perception of the social dimensions of our religious situation.

We shall take the liberty of relating these considerations to a frequently quoted passage from the New Testament—Jesus' injunction to His disciples to be "wise as serpents and innocent as doves" (Matthew 10:16). A brief investigation of the meaning of this passage may illustrate very clearly the point we are trying to make.

The passage is not taken out of context here. The writer of the Gospel places it in the context of Jesus' sending out of the twelve apostles. In other words, the passage concerns precisely the main subject matter of this essay—the mission of the Church in the world. Our immediate problem may be put in two questions. What is the "innocence" meant here? And what is the "wisdom?" The Greek word translated as "innocent" means, literally, "unmixed," "pure"; metaphorically, it means "simple," "without guile." The Greek word translated as "wise" means "sensible," "prudent," to be intelligent in a practical way. It is quite possible that allusion is made in this passage to a Jewish proverbial tradition ascribing these qualities to the two animals of the metaphor. A passage from later Jewish rabbinical literature is suggestive in this connection. A saying attributed to Rabbi Yehuda ben Shimon (fourth century A.D.) goes as follows: "God said regarding the Israelites: Towards me they are simple as doves, but towards the peoples of the world cunning as serpents."

This rabbinical saying may well be connected with the same proverbial tradition known to Jesus and the writer of the Gospel passage.

Whatever the final critical verdict on the passage may be, we would maintain that "innocence" here clearly does *not* refer to an intellectual quality. We would, incidentally, argue in the same vein concerning the use made of Jesus' various sayings about becoming like children to advocate an intellectual surrender to primitive credulity. It would seem rather that "innocence" refers to a quality of the heart, not the head—the purity of the heart that carries within itself and into a world of sin the message of God's love for men. One is reminded here of the title of one of Kierkegaard's discourses, "Purity of Heart is to Will One Thing."

"Innocence" is the upholding against all odds of the faith in God's love. And this "innocence," as the Greek word suggests, is "unmixed." It resists the constant temptation to "mix" this message of God's love with the messages of this world. If this is a correct interpretation, then our time is urgently in need of it, because we live in a period of intensive "mixing" (what scholars of religion have sometimes called "syncretism"). Thus, to be "innocent" means to reject the notion that the Gospel can be "mixed" with the message of psychological well-being or with the many messages of social order. The pure heart wills God and, therefore, wills truth. It wills nothing else. To identify the Gospel with mental health or with social progress is to "mix" it, to lose "innocence," to go against the meaning of Jesus' injunction in our passage.

But what is characteristic of our church life today is not "innocence" in this sense of religious passion; it is rather in the common American sense of the word "innocent" as a quality of being intellectually untouched, as a euphemism for plain ignorance or obtuseness, as another way of saying "born yesterday." Religion then becomes a starry-eyed optimism, a naïve credulity in the ideologies of the *status quo,* something that goes well together with an unthinking if benign conservatism in all areas of life. When all is said and done, religion then becomes a solemn ratification of an existence of trying to get along with a minimum of awareness. This is not only humanly reprehensible. It is an offense against the integrity of the Christian commitment.

A writer in the nineteenth century described the Church of England as the Conservative party gathered for prayer. There are many situations in which this statement would not be too inappropriate for our contemporary Protestant church life in America. On the campus, for example, the religious organizations are all too often the gathering place for the most conformist, the most anti-intellectual, the most prejudiced segments of the student population. And the view of society we find among our clergy and clericalized laymen is all too often a collection plate for every delusion to be found in the market. We would argue that such religiosity is something worse than mere intellectual sluggishness. There are many cases in which it offers the basis of a lifelong act of self-deception, of escape from the realities of existence—precisely what Sartre has called bad faith. But in the light of the sending out of Jesus' messengers it is something even worse than that. It is a betrayal of the Gospel.

When men follow Jesus' command to go out into the world as His messengers, they become bearers of the most priceless thing to be found in the world. With this mission they lose all rights to be "innocent" in the sense just mentioned. Relentless intellectual honesty becomes more than a matter of personal self-respect. It becomes part of the Christian mission.

In other words, the "wisdom" enjoined in our passage is directly related to the "innocence" enjoined just after it. To will God's love is to will truth. It is the immense responsibility for the Church's message which must compel the Church to perceive clearly the world into which this message must be carried. Nor is this something altogether new in the twentieth century. Clarity of perception is an essential ingredient of the entire prophetic tradition since the times of the Old Testament. The worship of the true God is always accompanied by the unmasking of idols. While it is important to keep apart these two actions (for the final address of God to man is not judgment but joy), it is worth while to keep in mind the place of such "negative thinking" in the economy of redemption.

Sociology has had such a debunking character from its inception. Sometimes this has been deliberate. At other times the sociologist has found himself playing a strange role of Balaam in reverse, setting out to praise and finding himself joining the chorus of those who would denounce. Again and again, the sociologist will find himself addressing those who would seek the truth in the clouds, pointing out to them what is to be found at their very feet, and telling them that this also is truth and that the truth of the sky must be reconciled with the truth as it exists on earth. It is no wonder that such inconvenient insistence is often brushed aside as puny-minded preoccupation with pedestrain matters. The sociologist will do well to continue insisting that the truth must be one. A truth which can reach the sky only by denying what exists on earth cannot be truth at all. It is a mystification. What is more, the sociologist can often point out that such mystification has behind it very good and very pedestrian motives indeed—namely, sociological motives.

We are probably justified in ascribing to the prophetic tradition of the Christian faith the capacity that the latter has shown to take great risks in the conviction that the truth must be one. The Thomistic enterprise of the Middle Ages was certainly an example of this, whatever we may say today about the philosophical validity of what it accomplished. Rightly or wrongly, it saw itself confronted with what appeared to be two truths— the truth of Christian revelation and the truth of Aristotelian philosophy. It was the courageous integrity of the Thomistic adventure which insisted that if indeed both of these were true, then there must be one single truth in which both could be reconciled; that reason and revelation could not be contradictory. An example somewhat closer to home would be the history of Biblical criticism within the Protestant tradition. It is a fact often overlooked that Biblical criticism, as we know it today, did not originate with the enemies of the Church. Its first great impetus as a scholarly discipline came from within the theological centers of learning of Protestant Germany. It is very likely that to Protestantism goes the honor of being the first in religious history to subject its own sacred writings to a merciless scientific scrutiny. Such an intellectual act of daring is again unthinkable without the confidence that God is truth and that, therefore, the man who faithfully pursues the truth will not find himself separated from God.

Sociological perception comes as a shock to the extent that it illuminates our real lives. Quite often it will lead us to seeing things in a new and surprising perspective. We would repeat once more our contention that Christian commitment involves a commitment to clear perception. It is only fair to add that the decision to see clearly at all cost may well lead to insights which destroy the various elements with which all of us seek to "mix" the Gospel—such as the delusion that the Christian faith is socially useful or acceptable. All the same, the writer would here state his belief that this process is akin to the working of acid on an alloy. That is, the sociological analysis of the religious situation may eventually help us to see more clearly what is the Gospel itself—that message of God's love which is entrusted to the care of the Church.

II

The Nature of
the Religious Establishment

1

The American Situation

It is a commonplace observation today that the world may be divided, irrespective of political allegiances, into "fully developed" and "underdeveloped" countries. In the interest of international politeness, the latter are now frequently referred to as "areas of rapid social change" (a term that has found special acceptability in ecumenical circles). This categorization, of course, is based primarily on the degree of economic and technological complexity attained by the countries in question. Thus we find in the first category the cluster of national societies in North America and western Europe aptly referred to as the "Atlantic community," as well as the Soviet Union and its European satellites and such individual countries as Australia and New Zealand and perhaps Japan and Israel. In the other category will be found the great bulk of the nations of Asia, Africa, and Latin America, embracing a wide variety of political and social characteristics, but all sharing the great gap which separates them economically and technologically from the societies in the first category. The overall effect of this perspective is to look upon the world as a struggle between the "haves" and the "have-nots." Therefore, despite all the din and clamor of the cold war, it would then appear that the Soviet Union and the United States have more in common in very important respects than the former has with China or either has with Indonesia. The crucial variable in any specific analysis under this perspective will always be the degree to which the society in question has been subjected to the radical forces of industrialization. Indeed, the most important fact in the world today is not some particular ideological alignment but the transforming power of the industrial revolution. Sociological interpretation in particular will be greatly affected by this perspective.[1]

Needless to say, this categorization is open to challenge, especially by those who place strong emphasis on political and ideological factors. It is not our purpose here to argue the merits of the matter. It is certainly possible to agree that this categorization has merits within limitations. However, we would issue a warning against a consequence often drawn from this categorization—namely, the notion that we must look to the "underdeveloped" countries if we want to find the clue to our future.

This notion finds expression in the reactions of American students who may be very much bored by investigations into their own society but develop strong interest in, say, what is happening in Indonesian society. Now we would readily grant that it is very important to understand what happens in Indonesia and that such happenings will strongly bear upon our own future, for instance in terms of the role played by the "underdeveloped" countries in the competition between ourselves and the Communist camp. The important point to make, however, is that our own society, much more than the Indonesian one, can give us clues concerning the future—or, at least, concerning a future that does not include a thermonuclear holocaust. It should not be difficult to see why this is so. As the industrial revolution engulfs wider and wider areas of our planet, the very forces are set in motion that have produced our own society and that of other "advanced" countries. It is not too much to say that, in this sense, America represents the future more than any other society

—simply because it is in America that the industrial revolution has gone furthest in transforming an entire culture. This has been aptly put in the original title of a book about America by a Swiss writer, Robert Jungk—*The Future Has Already Begun*. Thus, the so-called "Americanization" of western Europe is really a misnomer if it is understood as increasing American influence in that part of the world. What is happening, rather, is that a similar "affluent society" is coming into being on both sides of the Atlantic, with similar social effects on the entire culture. The similarity of much that is now taking place in the Soviet Union, a country hardly open to much American influence, is instructive in this connection. When Mort Sahl commented some time ago that the Russians have copied the organizational chart of the Strategic Air Command and even developed a guy who looks like General LeMay, he put his finger on a point that will bear considerable sociological analysis.

Nor is this view of America as the world's future something that emerges only from the arid abstractions of the sociologist. It is actually present in the dreams and aspirations of masses of people in the "underdeveloped" countries. Daniel Lerner has given us a vivid picture of this in his recent sociological study of the Middle East. Compare, for example, his description of the effects of American motion pictures on the grocer in a small Turkish village:

For the Grocer, movies were more than a homily on familiar themes. They were his avenue to the wider world of his dreams. It was in a movie that he had first glimpsed what a *real* grocery store could be like—"with walls made of iron sheets, top to floor and side to side, and on them standing myriads of round boxes, clean and all the same, dressed like soldiers in a great parade." This fleeting glimpse of what sounds like the Campbell Soup section of an A&P supermarket had provided the Grocer with an abiding image of how his fantasy world might look.[2]

Americans might well wish that this Turkish grocer would associate their country with things that they themselves regard as more important, such as their political convictions. But the fact remains that however unsuccessful America may have been in enlisting enthusiasm for its political goals in many parts of the world, it remains an image of economic and social well-being towards which millions aspire, so that even the Communists take the American standard of living as something to reach and eventually surpass. It may be much later, to their own surprise perhaps, that they will find themselves regaled not only with an American affluence of productivity but also with a very American problem of overproduction.

The foregoing remarks may be regarded as somewhat off the proper subject of this essay, except as they afford us a useful corrective against a common way of looking at American society —namely, looking at America as representing a static *status quo* in contrast to the turbulent dynamism of the "areas of rapid social change." As we have just suggested, such a way of looking is very misleading. Indeed, much of the dynamism of the "underdeveloped" countries comes from the stresses and strains of the industrialization processes which are pushing them in an "American" direction, in the sense of Lerner's analysis. Moreover, American society itself is the very opposite of static. Even if one may have reservations about the description "Permanent Revolution" applied to America by the editors of *Fortune* magazine, it is clear that American society continues to be dramatically transformed by a series of revolutionary forces. Before we look more closely at the role of religion in this society, it will be well if we at least cast a glimpse at these revolutionary forces. They form the indispensable background to any understanding of the religious situation.

The most obvious revolutionary force at work is technology itself, the gigantic power underlying industrialism, progressively invading and transforming every aspect of our culture.[3] What is most astonishing about our technological revolution is not only its progress but the increasing acceleration of that progress. While it took decades for technological developments to effect social change in the earlier period of the industrial revolution, far-reaching transformations may now occur within a few years after a new technological factor is introduced. Thus, one may compare the speed with which American society was changed by the introduction of railroads in the nineteenth century and that of the automobile in the twentieth. More recently, the effects of radio and television, respectively, afford another illustration of this. Sometimes the sociologists have a difficult time trying to keep up. While some sociologists are still pondering the role of the automobile in tearing apart the family as a social unit, others are pointing to television as a force pulling the family together again. And while some critics of our culture denounce the debasing influence of television, others hail the advent of high-fidelity recording as ushering in a new period of mass appreciation of good music. While it is in the economy that the immediate impact of technological forces is first felt, there is hardly a sector in our culture which is immune from this impact. Technology has revolutionized the processes of production and consumption. But it has also revolutionized the political order, the class system, the family, and even the area of morality. Totalitarianism could not have come into being without the instruments of mass repression and mass communication having been put into the hands of government by modern technology. But even intimate moral questions are grossly changed by technological developments. Sexual morality, for instance, takes on a completely new character in an age in which effective contraceptives are generally available and in which venereal disease can frequently be cured by a few injections of penicillin.

If the history of western culture in the century and a half preceding World War II cannot be understood without this ongoing technological revolution, what has been happening in the fifteen years since the end of the war is likely to bring about transformations of human life on our planet with which even an imagination nurtured on science fiction has difficulties in coping. Once more, it is American society that stands in the very center of these technological forces. It was in America that there rose on July

16, 1945, the first mushroom cloud of the atomic age. Perhaps the significance of this event is best stated in the words of a writer describing the reactions of the observers of this first atomic explosion:

It is a striking fact that none of those present reacted to the phenomenon so professionally as he had supposed he would. They all, even those— who constituted the majority—ordinarily without religious faith or even any inclination thereto, recounted their experiences in words derived from the linguistic fields of myth and theology. General Farrell, for example, states: "The whole country was lighted by a searing light with an intensity many times that of the midday sun. . . . Thirty seconds after the explosion came, first, the air blast pressing hard against the people and things, to be followed almost immediately by the strong, sustained, awesome roar which warned of doomsday and made us feel that we puny things were blasphemous to dare tamper with the forces heretofore reserved to the Almighty."[4]

It was at this moment that Robert Oppenheimer recalled a line from the Bhagavad-Gita: "I am become Death, the shatterer of worlds."[5]

While any reader of the daily newspapers can form an idea of the military possibilities of the atomic age, there are people who would argue that the developments now going on in electronics will have much more revolutionary consequences for our society if the peace is maintained. It is electronics rather than atomic energy which is bringing about the revolution of automation. We are only now beginning to see the consequences that automation will carry with it not only in our economy but in our society as a whole. Again, it is in America that these consequences are likely to be felt first. These considerations may suffice in giving us a sense of our technological revolution as it continues to gather momentum—even if we forego reflection upon the possible social consequences of the fact that we are now standing on the threshold of man's entry into space!

Closely related to the technological forces just mentioned is the revolutionary transformation of our economy aptly caught in

John Galbraith's phrase "The affluent society."[6] As Galbraith eloquently argues in his book of that title, America and the other "advanced societies" provide us with a spectacle totally new in human history—the spectacle of large masses of people living free from the immediate and constant burdens of grinding poverty, starvation, and deprivation of the elementary necessities of survival. This fact, to be found in all highly industrialized countries, constitutes an economic revolution of staggering significance. Contrary to a popular point of view in this country, this economic revolution cannot be explained by some peculiarly "American way of life," be it American democracy or American capitalism. The transforming power here is once more that of victorious industrialism, whether its victory occurs under the banners of socialism or under those of "free enterprise." America finds itself at the head of this revolution not because of its political institutions (which it shares with Costa Rica) or its capitalist system (which it shares with Portugal) but because of the triumphant development of an industrialism having at its base the immense physical and human resources of an entire continent.

The economic revolution relates to the technological one in what Gunnar Myrdal has called a "cumulative effect"—or, in other words, in the form of a vicious cycle, except that only a few would be disgruntled enough to call this relationship vicious. Industrialism is at the heart of the effect. Each technological advance makes possible a new abundance in the goods and services available to the "affluent society." In turn, as the standard of life keeps rising, its increasing demands stimulate further and further developments in the technology on which it is based.

The economic revolution has today engulfed just about the entire area of the continental United States, with only a few areas remaining what Galbraith has called "islands" of poverty. Needless to say, this does not mean that there are no more poor in America or even that soon there will be none. What it does mean is that even those who find themselves at the bottom of the affluence ladder have constantly before their eyes the promise

of a more abundant life—a promise which will often be broken
(as in the case of underprivileged minority groups) but which
will decisively color their aspirations, hopes, and plans. Within
this country the effects of the economic revolution on all aspects
of society can best be seen in the area affected by it most
recently—the South, rightly described today as America's "industrial frontier." The rapid rise in educational levels, the growth
of cities, the breakdown of the traditional political system, the
weakening of the caste patterns of racial relations, the decline
of such indices of "underdevelopment" as illiteracy, infant
mortality, and venereal disease—all these, directly or indirectly,
are part of the economic revolution producing a "new South"
and sucking it into the opulence of the national society.[7]

While the economic revolution of our "affluent society" has
gone far in eliminating certain age-old problems of the race, it
has engendered new problems of its own. There are multiform
consequences—to which we shall have occasion to return later
—to the fact that the orientation of our society has shifted from
production to consumption. There is the novel problem of overproduction, recently brought to public prominence by the discussion of "planned obsolescence."[8] There are the political and
social problems of the new forms of organization needed to
administer our gigantic economic machine—the complex termed
the "managerial revolution" by James Burnham.[9] There are the
problems, brought home in recent political controversy, of the
relationship of the private and public forces in the economy.[10]
In all these problems one thing remains most prominent—the
ever more rapid transformation of our society, often in directions
that we can but imperfectly foresee.

One of the most dramatic consequences of the technological
revolution has been the advance of medicine. Incidentally, this
is one consequence which has been felt even in countries with
very little industrial development, since modern medical techniques can be introduced rapidly even in a situation where the
bulk of the economy is still in a preindustrial stage. As a result
of modern medicine, diseases which were once the scourge of

mankind (such as bubonic plague) have been virtually wiped out and others (such as tuberculosis) have been reduced to controllable proportions. Every few years a new "miracle drug" or a new spectacular technique in surgery places another area of human pain under control. The most obvious result of this process has been that, even in the "underdeveloped" countries, disease rates have been declining and the average life expectancy has been steadily rising. While America does not have the highest health standards in the world (despite claims to the contrary by medical spokesmen), it finds itself here, too, among the most "affluent" societies. While it is naturally gratifying to reflect upon the fact that people today have an ever better chance of living healthier and longer lives than even their parents, let alone their grandparents, the most staggering social consequence of this fact has been less gratifying. We are referring, of course, to the so-called "population explosion."[11]

The basic cause of the astronomic rise of population all over the world today is not that people have more children, but that more of these children remain alive and that they live longer. Since, as we have mentioned, modern medicine can be effectively introduced into communities which otherwise may be quite untouched by modern technology or economic processes, the most spectacular (and frightening) increases in population are taking places in countries far down on the ladder of industrial development. But it would be a grave error to assume that the population problem exists only in China or India. It exists very much in the United States as well. Our population today is growing annually by about four million people—that is, by roughly the number of people in the city of Chicago. Even if we give credence to the claims of some business spokesmen who welcome our population growth as the opening of new internal markets for our production and, thus, a solution for many of our economic problems (a very dubious proposition), there are other consequences of this that are much less delightful to contemplate. Suffice it to mention here just the rapidly proceeding destruction of open land, the increasing difficulty of maintaining democratic processes in a society of such magnitude of population, and—ultimately the most important—the increasing ravaging of the natural resources of our continent.

Together the technological, economic, and demographic forces just enumerated have transformed the physical face of America. The rapid growth of cities, especially since World War II, is one of the best examples of this.[12] But it is not only the physical setting of our society that has thus been subjected to revolutionary forces. The social structure, the moral system, and perhaps even the psychological characteristics of the society have undergone profound and permanent changes. It is only as we become aware of these changes that we can achieve an adequate grasp of the dynamic character of the American situation.

The social revolution can be best seen by looking at what sociologists call stratification: in America this means essentially the class system.[13] Through most of history the stratification of a society, by whatever criteria one approached it, could best be depicted in the shape of a pyramid—the great bulk of the population being in the lower reaches of prestige and privilege, with fewer and fewer people involved as one goes up the social ladder. American society (as probably most "advanced" societies) is depicted more appropriately in the shape of a diamond, and it is in the middle strata that most of the people are to be found. One's conception of this will naturally vary with the categories of stratification one happens to be using. But there seems to be little doubt that the major effect of industrialism on stratification has been the steady expansion of the middle strata. In the societies living under western capitalism this process has been strikingly different from the one predicted by Marx. Rather than the proletariat becoming ever poorer and more numerous, it is the middle strata that have steadily expanded, with the total population steadily improving its standard of living.

American society is often described as "middle-class," and this has at least a double meaning. Its first meaning is that probably the majority of the American people thinks of itself as middle-class, including many people who by objective criteria such as income might be placed either higher or lower in the stratification system. Its second meaning is the pervasive influence throughout the entire culture of outlooks and values that have their origin in the middle strata. For example, the United States never developed a distinctive working-class culture similar to that which used to be found in European industrial countries. The essentially conservative character of the American labor movement is an expression of this. Most members of labor unions in America today have aspirations, convictions, and values only insignificantly different from those of their white-collar fellow citizens—and often have an income higher than that of the latter! This essential homogeneity of values has been greatly helped along by another aspect of the technological revolution—the impact of the mass-communications media, whose contents represent a standardized "American way of life" of middle-class character.[14] Regional and ethnic subcultures are rapidly being absorbed into this new national culture, supported by mass education and mass communications.

There are aspects of this social revolution upon which sociologists still disagree. There is, for instance, the question of whether social mobility (the movement of individuals and generations between the strata) has been increasing or diminishing. Or there is the question, discussed very much since the publication of C. Wright Mills' study of America's power structure, as to whether the democratic process is becoming increasingly ineffectual at the top of the social system.[15] But perhaps the most important consequence of the social revolution is the emergence of what Daniel Lerner (contrasting this with traditional societies) has called the "participant society."[16] Through most of human history the vast mass of the population did not consciously participate in the great social processes. These processes were, indeed, beyond the imagination of most of the people. History passed over them, was suffered by them, while their values and interests were limited by the narrow confines of their village or tribe. In contemporary American society nearly everyone is a participant—not, of course, in the sense of being in a position to shape significantly the course of events, but in the sense of being aware, having opinions, being able to "empathize" (Lerner) with those who make the important decisions. And this is true even where the awareness is distorted by propaganda or prejudice, or where the opinions are blatantly erroneous. This means, quite simply, that almost no one in our society is insulated from the vast transformations that are happening all around him. Not only is everyone a participant in fact, but he is also a participant in his own consciousness.

It should not surprise us, then, that American society has witnessed also what may well be called a moral revolution. As people's social horizons have widened, there has been a corresponding change (not necessarily for the better!) in their goals in life, and in their notions of right and wrong. Moreover, this change is closely related to the economic revolution. In a society where most of the necessities of life are scarce and sparsely distributed, it is only natural that moral approbation should be bestowed on such actions as promote production. In our society of abundance, those actions which promote consumption are increasingly granted moral ratification. This is at the heart of the transition from what William Whyte has called the "Protestant ethic" to the "social ethic."[17] In his classic sociological analyses, Max Weber has traced the development of "ascetic" values in western society—values that have been indispensable to the growth of industrial capitalism. There can be little doubt that American culture, despite all its Puritan vestiges, is veering away from such "asceticism." The ongoing struggle of the advertising industry with the remnants of a thrift-oriented economic ethic gives us a vivid picture of this—and the conviction that the advertisers are going to be successful![18] Whatever one might say ethically about this new mentality of happily wasteful indulgence, there can be little doubt that the latter is more functional in our economy of abundance than the old "ascetic" outlook of Yankee farmers and shopkeepers.

The pursuit of happiness has been an American ideal since the beginnings of the American republic. What has happened, however, is that the expectations of happiness as a goal to be achieved in one's own life have been steadily rising since the coming of the industrial revolution.[19] The coming into widespread acceptability of a hedonist sexual ethic is a good example of this process. Nor is it necessary to look at the more alluring data in the Kinsey reports to make this point. The rising divorce rates are as good for the purpose. It makes very little sense when these are looked upon as evidence of some sort of mysterious moral corruption. The divorce rates rather reflect two basic social processes, one economic, the other moral. The economic process is the one which, since the coming of industrialism, has transformed the family from a producing to a consuming unit, with the logical consequence that its ties have been weakening, since one will divest oneself much more easily from a fellow consumer than from a partner in production. The other process is a moral one—the victory of a moral ideal of marriage as a union of deep congeniality, an ideal which naturally raises very high all levels of expectation. Divorce is the expression of an indomitable hope in the future and of a stubborn conviction that happiness, in the fullest sense of the word, is not only possible but is one's inalienable right. Very likely all the other expressions of what Pitirim Sorokin has called the American "sex revolution" are to be understood in the same way.[20]

While we are looking at the revolutionary forces which are storming across the American scene, we might finally mention what is, at any rate, a plausible hypothesis—namely, that a new psychological type has been emerging in America in our century. Nor should this surprise us. It is, after all, a truism of social psychology that personality is directly related to the social structure. The most popular (and perhaps most ambitious) formulation of this hypothesis has been that of David Riesman—the idea that the American character has been shifting from the "inner-directed" to the "other-directed" type.[21] While Riesman's formulation is open to serious criticisms, it would seem clear that *something* has been happening to the prevailing American personality in our age. A personality functioning successfully in our abundant, highly organized, consumption-oriented society will have to be shaped differently from the personality that was at a premium, say, in the days of our grandparents. It would thus seem very probable that the revolutionary forces of our society not only transform our world but penetrate within ourselves as well.

Certainly it cannot have been our purpose in the foregoing paragraphs to give a thumbnail sketch of American society. Our purpose was simply to underscore the point with which we started this chapter. We find American society today in a complicated and dangerous international crisis, facing not only the Communist world as an avowed enemy but also the immense problems of the "underdeveloped" sectors of our planet. In looking outwards into these areas from our own vantage point and in being quite rightly impressed by the tremendous dynamism we perceive in them, it is rather easy to start thinking of our own society as a settled rock from which one may contemplate (be it with conceit, with sympathy, or with trepidation) a sea of troubles surrounding us. To do this, as we have suggested, is to overlook the dynamism inherent in our own situation. The ongoing American revolution is very different from the Chinese one or even the Indian one. But it is a revolution nonetheless.

It is against this background that we must try to understand the religious phenomenon in America. And, having attempted to understand it, it is against this same background that we must ask what the mission of the Christian Church ought to be in this society.

2

The Religious Paradox

Religion always exists within a certain historical and social situation. If nothing else, Biblical criticism has shown how important the understanding of this situation is for an understanding of any religious phenomenon, not only for science, but also for theology and faith. It goes without saying that the Christian will not be satisfied with understanding only. He will have to ask what this understanding means in terms of his faith and his mission in the world. But before he can ask these specifically Christian questions, he must clearly understand the situation within which he and his questions find themselves. We shall follow the same logical sequence in this essay. In this and the following chapters of this first part we shall seek to grasp the contours of the religious phenomenon in the American situation. We shall attempt to do so without reference to our own faith, hopes, or fears. In other words, in accordance with a "value-free" conception of social-scientific understanding, we shall ask what *is,* without immediately intruding into the analysis with our notions of what *ought* to be. The latter question we shall leave to the next part of this essay. The reader must be asked, therefore, not to be surprised if the writer speaks in rather different tones in these two parts of the essay. In this first part the writer will speak quite simply as a sociologist, with his Christian faith bracketed as firmly as is possible. It is in the next part that he will try to address himself to the situation analyzed as a concerned Christian. This procedure is not an indulgence in some sort of "double-think." It is rather an elementary requirement of intellectual honesty.

There can be little doubt about the prominence of the religious phenomenon in America. Religion occupies a conspicuous place in American society, is accorded considerable social prestige, and appears to be a matter of active interest to large numbers of people.[1] A newcomer to this country is likely to come to this conclusion even after a few weeks spent here, especially if he spends them in a smaller community. If he approaches the community by air, he may be struck by the number of spires reaching up towards him: it may even seem that there is one on every street in some towns! The newcomer will be impressed by the traffic congestion caused on Sunday mornings at the beginning and the conclusion of worship services. On Saturday the daily newspaper affords him a detailed prospectus of the "varieties of religious experience" that he might flavor on the following day. And it will not be long before one of his neighbors will ask him solicitously, "Have you decided yet on which church you want to join here?" If the newcomer comes from central or western Europe, he may wonder whether he has not come into a country which fulfils the wildest wish-thinking of his childhood's Sunday school teachers (it will depend on the individual case, of course, whether this wonder is one of pleasure or dismay).

There is also little doubt that this prominence of religion in American society is nothing new.[2] It was noted by European commentators, such as de Tocqueville, well over a century ago. It cannot be our concern in this essay to trace the historical causes of this place of religion in America. There is strong evidence, however, that there has come about in recent decades a further intensification of this American religiosity. We are referring, of course, to what has been called the postwar "religious revival."[3] In one sense this "revival" is nothing but the continuation of what statisticians call a "secular trend"—namely, the steady rise of church membership in America. We may look, for example, at the figures showing the percentage in the total population of church members over the last forty years:

1920: 43.0%
1930: 47.0%
1940: 49.0%
1950: 57.0%
1955: 60.9%[4]

And in 1960 the percentage was reported to have reached the two-thirds mark! Even though religious statistics are known for their lack of reliability, the over-all tendency here is well established.

However, the "religious revival" is more than the statistical growth of church membership. Since World War II, there has been a much more general increase in "religious interest" in America. It is indicated by the prominence of religious discussion in intellectual magazines,[5] the growing market for religious books, and the remarkable growth of religion departments in universities and colleges. Since the beginning of the first Eisenhower administration, there has also been a new intensity of religious rhetorics to be found in political life.[6] A conspicuous illustration of this has been the introduction of religious terminology into the oath of allegiance by nothing less than an act of the Congress. Moreover, as our afore-mentioned newcomer to America reads his newspaper, he can contemplate pictures of our national leaders weaving in and out of churches, opening their meetings with prayer, and posing reverently with Billy Graham. Next to such pictures he will find reiterated statements that the cold war is essentially a struggle between the deep religious values of the West (and especially, of course, of America) and the godless materialism of the Communists—often accompanied by the explicit reassurance that, this being so, Americans can count on the full support of the divinity being thrown in on their side.

We would contend that, despite considerable literature on the subject, there is still a need for thoroughgoing sociological investigations into the nature of this religious upswing. What is of importance for our purpose, however, is that the "religious revival" has put in sharper focus the more general features of the religious phenomenon in American society. As we go along in our attempt to understand this phenomenon, we shall have occasion to come back to and perhaps to engage in some speculation about the "revival." For the moment, we would emphasize one aspect of the religious scene which we have alluded to in the heading of this part of the essay—the existence of a *religious establishment* in America.[7]

We are deliberately using here the term which, in the English-speaking churches, has come to mean the kind of state-supported religion against which the Nonconformist movements were directed. Indeed, in a later chapter we shall argue that this term is valid even in its full political sense. At this point we would use the term in a somewhat broader sense—religion established securely and in a taken-for-granted manner as an important institution of American society. More than half the

American people identify themselves directly with the various religious denominations. A much larger number feel an implicit identification with them. Nearly everybody agrees that religion is a good thing and that it is important for the well-being of the nation. Indeed, the nation's leaders keep on maintaining that, in the last resort, religion is what America stands for. In the minds of many, to be a good American means *ipso facto* to have some kind of religious commitment—with the negative implication that the Americanism of the agnostic or atheist is open to challenge. The self-image of America is, indeed, "under God" (though, as we shall see, there are varying interpretations of what this means).

We are saying nothing new here. Actually we are simply repeating what our opinion-forming communications media tell us every day. And, though we shall reserve our interpretation of this statement for a while longer, we are willing to agree with this identification of America with religiosity. But in doing so we stumble at once upon a curious paradox, one that has been pointed out sharply by such observers as Reinhold Niebuhr and Will Herberg. This is the paradox that this religious establishment (and, for that matter, the religious renascence of recent decades) is to be found in a highly secularized society. The paradox crops up repeatedly in the pronouncements of the spokesmen of organized religion. On the one hand, these spokesmen may praise America for its religious stance and hold the country up as an example to the rest of the world. On the other hand, they may complain about what they themselves call the increasing secularization of American life. And once more we find ourselves agreeing, if not with the evaluation, at least with the description of the situation. When we probe what is meant by "secularization" in such statements, we find that the term refers to a segregation of religious motives within the religious institution itself. Within the broad areas of political, economic, and social life, religious motives appear to be of little relevance. The logic of policy and decision-making in these areas is overwhelmingly secular in character. Our religious spokesmen tell us that America is religious—and they are right, if they mean the prominence of the religious institution in the society. Our religious spokesmen tell us that America is secular—and they are right once more, if they mean that the religious institution exists in the society as a segregated enclave, surrounded by actions that have little if any relationship to religious motives. Often this interpretation of the facts is linked with the belief that things were very different in an earlier period of American history. Secularization then appears as a descent from a religious plateau to be located somewhere in the past. We may rightly be skeptical about such an assumption. But, be this as it may, the paradox of a religious establishment in a highly secular society is a reality of the present.

This segregation of organized religion from the dynamic forces of society can be illustrated by casting a glance backwards at the preceding chapter. One could say without risking much exaggeration that the religious institution is irrelevant in terms of any of the powerful revolutionary forces we mentioned there. A good example would be the relationship of Protestantism to the urban way of life.[8] In a society which is increasingly urban in character, Protestant churchmen tend to look upon the city as essentially their enemy. The virtues extolled from the pulpit are those appropriate to the countryside and the small town— in other words, to a way of life rapidly disappearing in America. Often enough this outlook is graphically depicted in the promotional literature concerning missionary ventures of the churches into this alien territory: there we can see a picture of a tranquil New England country church superimposed on another picture depicting an asymmetrical jumble of skyscrapers—Zion in the midst of the towers of Babylon. The modern world appears as a counterimage, often one of mystery that requires explanation and interpretation, usually one over which one laments the passing of a better day.

It is not surprising that, as a result, Protestantism has had little to say that would be of relevance to the mighty transformations through which American society has been passing.

Indeed, national denominational or interdenominational bodies, or the more socially conscious Protestant publications, might address themselves on occasion (some even with regularity) to timely issues. The local church, nevertheless, has generally remained in a defensive posture vis-à-vis the new America rising up around it. In our "affluent society," dominated by infinitely complex and gigantic organizations, churchmen have stood for the economic outlook of the small businessman. In a society in which a new and, in many ways, a revolutionary class system has sprung up, churchmen have commonly denied the reality of class altogether.

The difficulty which the local church has had in dealing with the young generation, especially with adolescents, is indicative of the yawning gap which separates it from the moral transformations of our time. We might take up the example of sexual morality once more. While the members of church-sponsored young people's groups are happily experimenting somewhere along the continuum from necking to petting to "the real thing," the official ideology continues to pretend that what goes on is all in the nature of "clean fun," as this concept might have been understood by a Y.M.C.A. secretary around the turn of the century. The young people in the case, for very understandable reasons, will co-operate in this game of self-deception. There then develops a double level of morality—the "official" one, which is practiced or pretended to in the presence of the religious "leaders," and the "unofficial" one, which is the self-understood reality as soon as these so-called "leaders" are off the scene. These latter, then, are genuinely surprised when the subterranean ethos, of which they were blissfully ignorant, sometimes comes irrevocably to the surface—as when one of their charges becomes pregnant or perhaps even tells them the truth in a moment of malicious honesty.

It is not our purpose here to discuss what a relevant Christian sexual ethic ought to be, and even less to say that the "unofficial" morality should be welcomed and recommended. Our point is rather that the local church, here as elsewhere, is effectively segregated from the real forces of our situation and thus finds itself unable to deal relevantly with this situation. Relevance presupposes a perception of the real situation. If such perception is present, it might be quite relevant to denounce with prophetic anger. In the absence of perception, however, it is only possible to uphold an ideology which is irrelevant to the facts of the matter. For the individual this generally means that he is left alone and without help in the moral choices he has to make.

Perhaps the crucial perception here—and one which is most generally lacking—is the perception of the segregation of the religious institution mentioned before. Since the religious institution is prominent and prosperous, it is only natural for the religious functionaries to assume that what they say and do has great impact on the lives of their people. The most common delusion in this area is the conviction of ministers that what they preach on Sunday has a direct influence on what their listeners do on Monday. This conviction, because it is so important for the self-image of the minister, is adhered to despite mountains of evidence to the contrary. The reality, of course, is that the person listening to the minister in church is a radically different one from the person who makes economic decisions the next day. When our typical church member leaves suburbia in the morning, he leaves behind him the person that played with the children, mowed the lawn, chatted with the neighbors—and went to church. His actions now become dominated by a radically different logic —the logic of business, industry, politics, or whatever other sector of public life the individual is related to. In this second life of his the church is totally absent. What the church has said to him might conceivably have bearing on his private life. But it is quite irrelevant to his involvement in public life. Indeed, the ideal suburban church member may, for all his minister is likely to know, derive his income from the most abandoned slum housing in the city. As soon as he steps outside the charmed circle of church, family, and suburban neighborhood, he may become a tyrant, a ruthless exploiter of men, a participant in any number of merciless conspiracies—and no one "back there" need ever know. At this point the religious segregation presents us with an interesting moral problem to which we shall have to return later, as it is of crucial importance to an understanding of our situation.

The paradox of religion in American society can thus be put in a slightly different form. On the one hand, religion appears as a prominent symbol of public life. On the other hand, for the individual, religion is relegated pretty exclusively to his private life—the hours of leisure in which he seeks refuge and repose from his involvements in public life. Religion as a national symbol—religion as a leisure-time activity: a curious paradox indeed!

We shall have ample occasion to ask what this paradox means from the viewpoint of the Christian faith. This is not yet our problem, though. The paradox calls not only for a Christian evaluation but also for a sociological understanding. For we are faced here with a curious fact from a purely sociological viewpoint as well. It is close to axiomatic for a sociologist that an institution which is prominent and accorded prestige in a society must, in some way, be functional to that society. This means that, in some way, it must fulfil a need, have social value, probably be conducive to the maintenance of the society in question. Behind the paradox we have just described, the sociologist will thus see another, an underlying paradox. We might call this the paradox of social functionality and social irrelevance. On the one hand, organized religion must be functional in American society; otherwise, it could not occupy within that society the place it now has. On the other hand, organized religion is irrelevant to the major social forces which are operative and determinative in American society: it does not affect them, and it relates to them in an overwhelmingly passive way. How is this possible? We shall attempt to answer this question in the next few chapters. We would already now contend that an understanding of what we have called the religious establishment in American society can give us the answer (that is, the sociological answer) to this question.

3

Cultural Religion

In a recent book about German Protestantism, Franklin Littell uses the term "nineteenth-century continuum" to describe the general assumption that religion and culture were part of one great harmonious whole (an assumption that received its severest jolt in the confrontation of the German churches with totalitarianism) and later goes on to say that the American churches today represent the last bastion of this "continuum."[1] We would contend that this term gives us an important clue to the social functionality of religion in America. It has many implications (not least political ones), but it may be most profitable to look at it first as it relates to what sociologists would call the "value system" of American society.

It is not necessary for our purposes to go into an elaborate discussion of different meanings attached to this concept. Essentially, what sociologists mean when they speak of "values" is pretty much what the man in the street would mean when he uses this word. The value system of a society defines for its members which goals they should aspire to and also provides them with criteria to distinguish "good" conduct from "bad." The words "good" and "bad" are put in quotation marks here not to cast doubt on the possibility of ethical judgment but simply to point out that different societies or social groups may put quite conflicting evaluations on identical actions. As Pascal pointed out long ago, what is truth on one side of the Pyrenees may be error on the other. The concern of the sociologist, as a sociologist, is not to decide the issue but to provide an objective analysis of the way in which the two beliefs are grounded in the two distinct societies which adhere to them. It goes without saying that such analysis of values is very important if one is to understand any society.[2]

It also goes without saying that in a society as complex and populous as America there will be divergent values among different groups and even situations in which values might clash sharply. Nevertheless, American society, or any other, could not function unless there were at least a degree of consensus about values crucial to the ongoing life of the society. There is evidence, however, that this consensus is much more than a minimal one, so that it is actually possible to analyze American society as having a high degree of cohesion and consistency in terms of its values.[3] Perhaps the classical account of this consensus in American sociology is found in the second study of "Middletown" by Robert and Helen Lynd.[4] In describing what they called "the Middletown spirit," the Lynds used the happy term "of-course statements" to refer to those values of the community about which consensus was so strong that any question regarding them would likely be answered with an "of course!"—so much so that the mental balance of the doubter would be open to challenge. The Lynds were studying a midwestern community in the mid-1930s, but we are on safe ground if we argue that since then, if anything, the cohesion of the American value system has increased rather than decreased. We would once more refer in this connection to the impact of the new media of mass communications, functioning as immensely powerful molders of consensus throughout the society.

The Lynds also have defined very clearly the relationship of the religious institution to this consensus: "To Middletown the role of religion is not to raise troublesome questions and to force attention to disparities between values and current practice."[5] Instead, religion supports and guarantees the value system of the community, and "going to church becomes a kind of moral life-insurance policy."[6] What does this mean? Its meaning is very simple. The religious institution does not (perhaps one should say "not any longer") generate its own values; instead, it ratifies and sanctifies the values prevalent in the general community. There is little if any difference between the values propagated by the religious institution and those of any secular institution of equivalent status in the community (such as the school). In Littell's meaning of the word, there is a continuum of values between the churches and the general community. What distinguishes the handling of these values in the churches is mainly the heavier dosage of religious vocabulary involved. But even here the churches are not sharply differentiated from, say, the educational or political institutions, which also employ a heavily religious rhetoric. Another way of putting this is to say that the churches operate with secular values while the secular institutions are permeated with religious terminology. In both cases, the terminology is derived from the often referred to Judaeo-Christian tradition, though it has been radically voided of the religious contents it possessed in this tradition. The terminology now applies to a vague religiosity which Will Herberg has called the "common faith"[7] and Martin Marty has described as "religion-in-general."[8] Since this religiosity is held both within and without the religious institution proper, an objective observer is hard put to tell the difference (at least in terms of values affirmed) between the church members and those who maintain an "unchurched" status. Usually the most that can be said is that the church members hold the same values as everybody else, but with more emphatic solemnity. Thus, church membership in no way means adherence to a set of values at variance with those of the general society; rather, it means a stronger and more explicitly religious affirmation of the same values held by the community at large.

We shall have occasion later to ask what this value continuum implies for the personal meaning that religion will tend to have in this situation. We may now ask in somewhat more detail what the characteristics of this "common faith" are and how they relate to specific American values. What we have to say here will follow rather closely the perceptive analysis of this made by Will Herberg.[9]

Perhaps the most striking characteristic of this "common faith" is its intense this-wordliness. This will hardly come as a surprise to those familiar with Max Weber's classic study of the this-wordly ethic of Protestantism, especially in the Calvinist form of it which became most formative in America.[10] However, there is an important difference between the early Protestant developments in which Weber was interested and the contemporary "common faith." In the former case, the ethical emphasis was indeed this-wordly (in contrast to medieval Catholicism, with its depreciation of secular activities); but this ethic was meaningful only against a background of intense preoccupation with supernatural realities. Today, the supernatural has receded into a remote hinterland of consciousness, mainly to break forth in moments of personal crisis, while the this-wordly ethic has remained with a vengeance. Indeed, if religion were to be identified with some sort of preoccupation with the supernatural, then what is said and done in most of our churches can hardly be given that name at all. The concern is not man's relationship with the divinity, but his relations with others and perhaps with himself. In other words, religion becomes in the main a matter of morals and psychology. It is this world which matters, not a world to come. The supernatural remains somehow taken for granted, but not as one's principal concern; rather, it is perhaps something to fall back upon in case of need. Even prayer itself, that audacious attempt of man to address one utterly beyond human measure, becomes typically an occasion of moral preachment or of psychological manipulation. Since the interest is almost exclusively moral and psychological, there is little interest in an intellectual grappling with the problem of religion. Not only in the laity, but with amazing frequency among the clergy as well, theology is rather a bad word, something that one may leave to eccentric seminary professors but that has little relevance to the ongoing business of both corporate and individual religious life. Religion thus becomes a matter of conscience and of emotion, segregated from the activities of intellect.

Again, it would be interesting to investigate the historical process by which this state of affairs came about. For our purposes, however, an understanding of our contemporary configuration is quite sufficient. We may now clarify the latter with the help of some specific examples of American values.

Possibly one of the most commonly held American values is that of success competitively achieved. Our entire educational system advocates it. Even very small children learn to play competitive games as individuals or teams. And everyone accepts this value as a valid explanation of a wide variety of actions. It explains why a man must sometimes be ruthless in getting ahead in his chosen career. And it explains why his girl might leave him if he has given up trying. "The best man wins"—in love, in business, and even in the world of learning. To deny the successful winner the spoils of his effort or to fail while aspiring towards a similar success is failure in its most un-American form. A stranger to America who had perhaps read something in the New Testament about the lilies of the field and similar matters might expect that the Christian churches would find themselves in sharp tension with this value. But he will find that the very opposite is the case. The churches hardly lag behind the schools and the business world in urging success upon those who are its members. They might possibly emphasize a little more strongly that success is to be achieved within morally permissible bounds, but the best argument made by them for morality itself is that it does not hinder success and might even help in achieving it. What is more, the same value dominates within the religious institution itself. There are successful ministers and unsuccessful ones. The criteria of success may vary slightly from those of the businessman (though sometimes the variation is embarrassingly slight!), but the goal is still there.

Some time ago a sociologist had an interesting conversation with a Protestant minister in the South. The context of the conversation was the minister's deploring of the alleged fact that today's youth has become soft and without enterprise. But, said the minister, there were still encouraging exceptions. To illustrate this, he told the story of a young man who had come out of military service and had set up a small business in the town. He worked at it very hard and in a short time he had driven his principal competitor, a much older man, into bankruptcy. The point of the story was to describe a fine young man. By contrast, it would be interesting to ask how this story would be evaluated by a religious spokesman (say, a Catholic priest in southern Italy) in a culture where competitive achievement was not a taken-for-granted good.[11]

Another central American value is that of activism. Americans in all walks of life pride themselves on being "doers." With this extolling of activity goes logically a depreciation of the contemplative life. The dreamer, the mystic, the single-minded thinker, the poet—all these have been marginal figures in American culture, a state of affairs caught well in Raymond Aron's description of America as the "hell of the intellectuals." Again, this can be seen most clearly by comparing America with cultures where different values are prominent. The *shtetl* culture of east-European Jewry would be a good case in point. Here the contemplative life, as expressed in the existence of the scholar, was the highest possible value. And so it might happen frequently that a wealthy merchant would be happy to marry off his daughter to an impecunious rabbinical student. With the dowry, the young wife would set up a little store and work in it all day long to support a growing family—and the husband would continue a full-time life of learning at the *shul,* grateful that he no longer had to worry about his material sustenance. The motives of the husband might be readily understandable to contemporary American males working themselves to an early grave to support their heavily mortgaged suburban ménage. There is hardly an American girl, Jewish or gentile, who could reproduce the simple satisfaction of thus being able to do her small part in the service of scholarship!

Again, an alien observer might expect there to be considerable tension on this point between the religious institution and the general culture. But, again, he will find that there is no tension at all, at least within the Protestant camp, which is our main concern here. The churches also pride themselves on their activity, their practical-mindedness, and their realistic coping with problems that "one can do something about." The life of prayer and theological learning is relegated to experts, who might occasionally "inspire" others by their discourses on these subjects. These experts, however, are vicarious rather than exemplary. It is understood that the average church member, as well as the average religious functionary, has little time for such eccentricities. Thus, the intellectual in the religious institution is as much a marginal man as he is in the culture at large. Seminaries for the training of religious functionaries, with some noteworthy exceptions, are frankly "professional schools"—which simply means that they train their students how to operate effectively within the religious institution with a minimum of intellectual preparation. Theology, at best, then becomes a professional ideology very much in the same way as some sort of patriotism is necessary for the professional soldier as a rationalization of *his* activity. If the contemplative life of the intellect is marginal to the religious institution, that of the mystic is normally beyond the range of possibility. It would require a good satirical pen indeed to describe the embarrassment that would be caused in one of our Protestant seminaries or church gatherings by the appearance of anyone claiming to have had a genuine encounter with the supernatural. Such an emergency, however, has become quite unlikely with the psychiatric screening and counseling procedures that have become commonly accepted in our ecclesiastical institutions!

Another prominent American value that we might mention here is that of social adjustment. In its contemporary form, this value finds its expression in what Riesman has called the "other-directed character" and Whyte the "organization man"—in other words, in the sort of person who will get along well in the large bureaucratic structures that dominate most of our life today. Adjustment to this situation today puts a premium on quite distinctive personality traits—an ability to get along with all sorts of people above and below oneself in a hierarchy; the willingness to submerge one's own strong views or, even better, not to have any; a suppression of tendencies towards irony or radical criticism; a readiness to identify fully with whatever group the exigencies of life have led one to affiliate with; and a further readiness to involve in this adjustment not only oneself but also one's family and friends.

Here also, despite the prophetic tradition so prominent in the Bible, we find the churches in broad consensus on this value. It is true that some degree of personal peculiarity may be permitted a minister, especially in the pulpit, but the most successful ministers in the eyes of their flock are still those who manage to be "regular guys." This is even true in the way in which ministers themselves look upon each other. In our middle-class Protestant churches, criteria of social acceptability among the clergy are increasingly similar to those existing in the world of the other—the nonreligious—organizations. Only recently a seminary professor remarked to the writer that undergraduates who will not attend collegiate football games are hardly the sort of people he would want to see in theological education. And the desirability of a new minister was expressed to the writer on another occasion by the observation that the man in question had an attractive wife and could tell a slightly off-color joke. It needs very little social-psychological sophistication to see that when such personality traits are at a premium in an institution they will rapidly come to dominate among the personnel of that institution.[12] Where psychological tests, constructed around such criteria of desirable personality traits, are used to screen prospective personnel, the selectivity becomes even sharper.

More is involved here, however, than the cultivation of ec-clesiastical "men in gray flannel suits." The rejection of the rebel, the eccentric, and the nonconformist implies not only a personnel policy but also an entire view of the social world. Since one ought fundamentally to adjust to society, this means that society is fundamentally good—our society, that is. Here and there one might want to make a few corrections and iron out some difficulties. But the main approach to the social world is one of affirming the *status quo* and of seeking to harmonize whatever forces tend to disturb it. Thus (again speaking of middle-class Protestantism), one is opposed to conflict and in favor of peace on the social scene. The important point to grasp here is that this bias towards harmony operates regardless of what the situation may be. In situations of industrial conflict one will advocate the re-establishment of peace—which, of course, means the return to the *status quo ante*. In situations of racial conflict the same tendency will prevail—which here means that the system of racial segregation or discrimination receives the designation of peace, while the forces which seek to disrupt the system become seen as disturbers of that peace (as, naturally, they are). In other words, the value of social adjustment frequently involves an implicit conservative viewpoint. Social reality is seen as a harmonious equilibrium and social ethics is concentrated on the disturbances of that equilibrium. Thus, one sees ethical problems in divorce but not in marriage, in crime but not in the law, in rebellion rather than in conformity. Quite apart from what this viewpoint may mean in terms of the Christian faith, it should be obvious that it brings about a highly selective perception of the social world.

There are some cultures in which the metaphysical dimensions of human existence (such as death, evil, passion in all its forms) are recognized and maintained in consciousness. There are others in which these dimensions are suppressed as much as possible. Within western civilization, Spain might be taken as an example of the former—in that respect a polar opposite of America. For, if human existence could be said to have a day side and a night side, then American values strongly emphasize the former against the latter. In this respect, American culture has a rather striking resemblance to that of Confucianist China, where the metaphysical concerns were also suppressed in the sane, sensible conduct of one's practical life.[18] Such a cultural "way of the middle" (to use a Confucianist term) will attempt to avoid any experiences of ecstasy, that is, any experiences where men may step outside the routine of everyday life and confront the terrors of their condition. This characteristic of our culture is expressed very clearly in our funeral customs.[14] The procedures, terminology, and professional ideology of the mortician's trade in this country all revolve around one fundamental aim—the camouflage of the reality of death. Nor could this be otherwise in a culture which bids men always to look upon the bright, daylight side of things. Death cannot be faced and therefore must be denied. But the denial of metaphysical concerns is not limited to the extreme fact of death. Our culture shields us effectively from all visible signs of suffering and degradation. Many of us go through life without seeing anyone die, let alone be born. Pain is quarantined in hospitals and social-work agencies. Poverty can be avoided by those whose cars travel quickly from the suburbs to the inner city over speedways cutting right through festering slums. Even our executions are performed in secret with the sterilized efficiency of scientific methods of murder, such as the electric chair and the gas chamber. Thus, an American child growing up in suburbia today has an uncanny resemblance to the young Buddha whose parents shielded him from any sight involving human suffering and death. To suggest that such a way of life may have serious deficiencies is commonly brushed aside as neurotic; the poet and the prophet, who may shrilly point to the darkness surrounding our clean, little toy villages, quite naturally are regarded as candidates for psychotherapy. And psychotherapy itself sees its aim in the restoration of the "way of the middle," which the culture espouses. Both passion and evil then become forms of pathology.

It is rather a difficult feat to operate a religious establishment which exists without tension in this culture. For religion, after all, has from time immemorial been concerned with the facts of evil, suffering, and death. Yet the American religious establishment, especially in its Protestant core, has succeeded in minimizing these elements to a remarkable degree. Perhaps once again we might look for an explanation of this to the innerwordly tendency of Calvinist Protestantism. Be this as it may, a religion which concentrates on moral conduct and mental consolation can dispense with the metaphysical dimension of human existence. The religious establishment, too, buttresses the values of the "way of the middle." Perhaps the phrase "all this and heaven too" puts rather succinctly the relationship of religion to the pervasive optimism of American culture.

If we then see the religious establishment as a predominantly passive expression of the American value system, we would expect that changes in the latter will naturally bring about changes in the former. While we cannot go into an exhaustive analysis of this here, we would contend that there is plenty of evidence that this is just what happens. A good case in point would be the decline of the old Protestant ethic and the rise of a new "social ethic," as discussed by William Whyte.[15] This change can be interpreted sociologically rather easily as logical in the transition of a society whose main problem is production to one oriented towards consumption. The traditional values of rugged individualism, ascetic hard work, and thrift become obsolete in this transition. Their place is taken by the conformity and hedonism which are today the boon (and, at least in part, the product) of the advertising industry. What is so interesting, however, is the way in which religion follows this over-all cultural trend. While the lower-class churches commonly represent the old ethical values, the middle-class churches (especially in suburbia) reflect faithfully the new morality, as Whyte shows sharply in his analysis of the religion of the "organization man." To explain this by the difference between a fundamentalist and a more liberal theology would be putting the cart before the horse. The sociologist will point out that the lower classes are still the most segregated from the new affluence, which has its principal locale in middle-class suburbia. It is not surprising, then, that the ethical emphases of religion in those two areas of our society vary accordingly. The self-interpretation of many of our middle-class churches actually states this situation explicitly. If the churches are understood as institutions designed to satisfy "religious needs," it is logical that their character will change in accordance with the needs of their constituency. One might point here to the ideology of religious education as an excellent illustration of this. The old Protestant ethic ratified (and historically probably created) the values of a young, vigorous industrialism bent on production. The new Protestantism validates the values of an industrial society that has become mature and settles down to consume happily what its huge economic machine restlessly produces. The churches function in this new society as the integrators and propagators of a common cultural religion.

In the preceding pages we have found it necessary to say several times that our remarks refer principally to middle-class Protestantism. It is this group of churches, which Carl Mayer has called the "central core" of American Protestantism,[16] with which we shall be mainly concerned throughout this essay. These churches are those descended, in one way or another, from the Calvinist or Arminian branches of the Reformation, even if sometimes (as in the Methodist case) the descent is of an indirect nature. It is these churches which occupy the center of the Protestant scene in both numbers and influence. To their "left," we find the various sectarian movements, largely lower-class in constituency; to their "right," the churches in the liturgical tradition (that is, the Episcopalians and the Lutherans), today mainly middle-class and above in social standing. We would contend that this "central core" is the main locale of the cultural religion discussed here. Here the fusion between religion and culture is strongest, for historically understandable reasons. This is certainly not to say that *only* in these churches is such a fusion to be found. The lower-class religious groups, as we shall see later, also relate to the culture in a very distinctive way. And there has been a very strong influence by these centrally located churches not only on American Anglicanism and Lutheranism but also on any major religious group now existing in this country. Thus, Will Herberg argues convincingly that American Catholicism and Judaism have also been strongly affected by the "common faith" of the society. Nevertheless, in terms of the American cultural religion, it is in the churches outside the "central core" that the strongest "countervailing movements" are to be found, to use a term recently applied in a slightly different sense by Robert Lee.[17] Perhaps American Protestants, who are concerned with this fusion of culture and religion, might do well to ponder whether they do not owe a measure of gratitude to Catholicism, which, despite all the Americanization it has undergone, has remained in a state of tension with the over-all culture—and thus provides an important witness to religion that is not simply a reflection of secular values.

With the reservations just made, we have now brought into focus what is probably the most important social function of religion in America—the function of symbolic integration. Those familiar with Emile Durkheim's sociology of religion[18] or with the functionalist approach to religion[19] will quickly identify this concept with a much broader theory. The general viewpoint of such a theory would be that religion, especially through its solidarity-generating symbols, functions to integrate and maintain society. For those concerned with relating our remarks here with broader sociological generalizations, the writer would state that he has considerable reservations about this viewpoint, certainly in its classical Durkheimian formulation. It is true that religion functions to integrate societies. It is probably true that this is the way in which religion functions most of the time. However, a sociological theory of religion must be capable of including within it those cases in which religion serves to *dis*integrate society, where its relationship to society is not functional but *dis*functional. This essay is not the place for a theoretical elaboration of this problem. Suffice it to say that we are not interested here in arguing that religion *always* acts to "symbolically integrate" society. What we are contending is simply that it does so *in America*.

Whatever the function of religion may be in other situations, we would thus contend that the following description of the integrative function of religion made by J. Milton Yinger applies very well to American society and especially well to Protestantism in that society:

Social order requires a unifying value scheme, specifying approved means and ends, to hold in check the conflict involved in the individual pursuit of scarce values and the hostility generated by the frustrations and disappointments of life. . . .

Religion may, under some circumstances, help to solve the problem of order, both as a designator of goals (with particular emphasis on shared goals), and as an enforcer of means. By ritual, by symbol, by its system of beliefs, its doctrines of rewards and punishments, religion may help to produce the socialized individuals who accept the dominate values as to legitimate means and ends.[20]

It should be obvious that, under these circumstances, religion will be primarily conservative in character. It will seek to maintain what social structures exist rather than to innovate or produce new structures. Its ideal will be some sort of social harmony, the dimensions of which are already given in the *status quo*. It will tend to think of society in a quasi-organic way, with the ideal being an equilibrium of social forces. This notion of equilibrium, coupled with the idea of the continuum of values discussed before, is expressed well in the phrase "religious-secular balance," recently used by Talcott Parsons to describe the religious situation in America.[21]

If one sees American religion in this perspective, it is hardly flattering but quite understandable if one begins to think in anthropological terms. The thought of primitive societies, with their taboos and totemism, begins to obtrude rather forcefully. The figure of the modern religious functionary solemnly sanctifying the values of society begins to have a disturbing similarity to the shaman twirling the sacred rattles as the tribe goes about its ceremonial dances. This perspective is well expressed in W. Lloyd Warner's analysis of Memorial Day ceremonies, of which we shall quote only the following characteristic paragraph:

Just as the totemic symbol system of the Australians represents the idealized clan, and the African ancestral worship symbolizes the family and state, so Memorial Day rites symbolize and express the sentiments of the people for the total community and the state. But in so doing, the separate values and ideas of various parts of the community are also portrayed. The ideas and values of several religions, ethnic groups, classes, associations, and other groupings are symbolically expressed and their place within the social structure of the community clearly indicated.[22]

Amid this symbolic apparatus religion occupies a central place. It affirms the legitimacy of the other symbols and integrates them into a sacred whole. It is thus very logical that religious functionaries occupy an important place in all community ceremonies of this kind.[23]

While we shall postpone to the next chapter the political implications of this integrative function of religion, there is one further aspect of this that we still ought to look at here. This is the aspect of ideology. Ideology is a term used somewhat ambiguously by various sociologists. We employ it here in the very specific sense of a set of ideas serving the vested interests of a particular social group. In this sense, ideology may be described as the sociological parallel to the psychological concept of rationalization. And in a way very similar to this psychological process, ideology commonly involves a distorted view of reality. Now, symbolic integration does not necessarily have to be ideological. For instance, the well-nigh universal religious validation of the incest taboo is certainly functional in the sense of the integration of society, but it hardly represents the vested interests of a particular social group. If, on the other hand, a group of priests should claim divine sanction to enjoy sexual privileges denied to others, one may say that the religious ideas supporting this view are ideological in character. In terms of our situation, when we say that religion functions to "symbolically integrate" society, this does not necessarily imply that religion is ideological. But there are cases where this statement may be made. These cases are worth at least a brief look.

One of the best recent studies of religion operating ideologically is the study of a small rural community in upstate New York by Arthur Vidich and Joseph Bensman.[24] It is already revealing that religion is discussed in the part of the study headed "The Reconciliation of Symbolic Appearances and Institutional Realities." The burden of the entire study is the absorption of the old culture of small-town America into the dynamism of modern mass society. The old economic, political and social institutions of the rural community are rapidly disintegrating under the impact of these new forces. As in all situations of rapid social change, this is a process accompanied by much anxiety and frustration. In this process the old ethos and the old values take on the character of an ideology. They are maintained in the act of denying the transformation that is occurring. They allow the individual to keep hold of a perspective on his existence that no longer corresponds to the facts. Thus, a gap opens up between the symbolic forms and the social realities of the community. One may say, of course, that such mild delusion is itself quite functional, insofar as it makes the transition from one social form to another easier for the individuals in question. This, however, does not change the analysis of what is going on. While the study of the community, which the authors have called Springdale, has many important sociological implications, the one which is most important for us here is the one concerning religion. For the churches of Springdale appear as the principal agencies in the community through which the ideology is maintained. To quote the authors: "Religion serves to accentuate and emphasize the public values of the community and to surround those values with a framework of church activity which further accentuates participation in and commitment to those values."[25] The sum total of these values is what the authors call the "public ideology," which systematically prevents the tensions of the real social situation from being verbalized. The churches perform a key part as ceremonial agencies that publicly proclaim what the community is not and would like to be:

Public meetings serve as ceremonial occasions at which all of the illusions enunciated reflect the public ideology. In light of the tenacity with which the exponents of the public ideology cling to it, it becomes understandable why it is possible to hear day after day and week after week what to an outsider appears to be an endless repetition of highsounding clichés and sentimental rhetoric. The dominant, publicly repeated ideology proclaims Springdale to be "a wholesome friendly place, the best place to bring up children, and made up of ordinary people, just folks, trying to make their community a better place to live. Nobody here has to worry about having friends, all you have to do is to be friendly yourself. No problems are too big for Springdale, it's the outsiders that cause all the trouble. People here have a lot of community spirit, you can always get people to take part, but usually the busiest people are the most reliable. One thing about Springdale, nobody is excluded, this is a democratic town. Anybody who tries to run things gets pushed down, but fast. If you join clubs you can learn things and have a lot of fun too. Everybody was invited and fun was had by all."[26]

The bulk of the Springdale study shows point by point how the reality of the community is pretty close to being the opposite of what this idyllic statement claims it to be. And it is no accident that each point in the above statement could be taken from a typical sermon preached in typical churches in communities just like the one of this study.

Yet the ideological function of religion is not limited to the sort of small town that Vidich and Bensman were interested in. It is equally in evidence in suburbia. While the small-town church adheres to an image of a reality no longer present, the suburban church upholds an image that never existed at all. This image, of course, is the suburban myth itself, which has been analyzed by such observers as A. C. Spectorsky,[27] William Whyte, and the team that produced the classic study of the Canadian community called Crestwood Heights.[28] The ideological aspects found in Springdale may be found in suburbia as well, despite the greater sophistication about the world to be found in the latter. As Maurice Stein put it in his discussion of the Springdale study:

The myth of local autonomy is not peculiar to the small town though it is not usually as central an aspect of community ideology. The distinctive feature is the organization of community affairs around this myth to a point where the defense of this illusion entails serious impairment of symbolic functioning. . . . The exurbanites are at the opposite pole of Springdale in one respect—they are painfully aware of their subordination to technical roles in mass society. Their movement to the exurbs involved a response to the constrictions imposed by these roles. They sought a synthesis of rural and urban values but found themselves plunged even more deeply into the "rat race" because of the heavy expenses required to maintain their rural facilities. . . . Their adjustment takes the form of institutionalized "cynicism" which contrasts sharply with the institutionalized "naïveté" of the small town. This cynical posture allows them to feel that they are distinctive because they know the real truth about modern society and therefore are superior to the "suckers" who have not seen through the disguise. Despite their "cynical" masks, many exurbanites cherish a secret dream of turning to "creative" jobs. But their mounting indebtedness keeps pace with their rising salaries to eliminate this as a realistic possibility.[29]

While we would agree with Stein's evaluation of the suburban "cynicism," we would emphasize the degree to which the "rural" dream of this frustrated exodus from the "rat race" is maintained within suburbia. Stein is probably correct in observing that this ideology is less naïvely believed in than the corresponding one of the small town. But it is there all the same. And, once more, the suburban churches play an important part in maintaining it.

One may look here, for instance, at the old village churches in New England communities, once rural in character and now becoming engulfed in the metropolitan "explosion." Of all the institutions in these new suburbs, the churches stand out as symbols of a way of life which has passed—and in search of which the new residents have come to live there. We find here the same features that characterized the ideology of Springdale: the notion of a warm, simple, neighborliness; the illusion of independence; the denial of competition and conflict; the dream of living a creative and perhaps even individualistic life in the bosom of the family—the whole package given religious sanction and emphasis by the churches. Indeed, it may well be that in many cases the act of joining one of these churches (often the first religious affiliation in the life of the individuals in question) is itself an affirmation of the dream. The segregation of the religious institution from the pressures of the situation from which people try to escape to suburbia naturally serves to foster this ideological function. Thus, as the mortgages pile up and the ulcers keep growing, one mows one's lawn, gossips with the neighbors—and goes to worship in the whitewashed monuments of an idealized past.

While religion can integrate societies existing with little stress and strain, it is most likely to become ideological when the latter begin to appear. Ideology now becomes an institutionalized manipulation of anxieties. We might elaborate here and discuss how religion may become ideological in other cases where social groups feel threatened by change. An interesting topic would be the analysis of religious factors in the conservative ideology employed by American business groups that feel threatened by the rapid economic changes of our society. Another intriguing subject would be the religious aspects of the self-delusions often involved in the international posture of this country, when the divinity is dragged in to give reassurance in a situation where few realistic comforts are to be found. This, however, is not necessary for our present purpose. It is enough to have pointed to the ideological function as a possible amplification to the general function of symbolic integration. As religion generally supplies integrating ideas for our society, in certain cases this service has to be reinforced by a dose of illusion. While this latter addition is not universal, it remains a possibility inherent in the continuum of values we discussed. Cultural religion is always at least potentially ideological. The understanding of this possibility is necessary if we are to perceive the situation clearly.

4

Political Religion

In discussing the function of symbolic integration carried on by the churches in American society, we have already made several references to the political implications of this. It is now our task to make explicit this relationship between the religious and political institutions. In doing so it will be not so much a question of introducing new material as a question of drawing the political implications out of what we have already discussed. The reason for this is quite simply that the political character of American religion becomes clear once the continuum of values between the churches and the secular society is fully grasped. We can then see that the term "establishment" is much more than a sociological metaphor. It refers to very much the same situation with which it has been associated in Europe—the intimate relationship between religion and the state.

Every American school child knows that one of our basic principles is the separation of church and state.[1] The Presidential campaign of 1960 has given everybody, Republican or Democrat, Protestant or Catholic, an opportunity to reiterate this elementary civics lesson on every political platform in the country. It is noteworthy that practically nobody questioned whether this separation now exists; the controversy was over the question of whether the election of a Catholic to the Presidency would endanger its continued existence. We would contend that, quite apart from the political irrelevance of the entire controversy, the actual reality of the relationship between religion and politics in America was missed by almost all parties in the case. And we would contend further that in reality this separation—so fervently proclaimed by liberal constitutional lawyers, Southern Baptist demagogues, and polite Jesuit apologians—is at best a very precarious myth. The real question is not the separation of church and state. It is rather the question of the character and delimitation of a state religion, which most of us affirm without being fully conscious of what it is that we are affirming.

As in many other cases of social analysis, our vision here is commonly clouded by a fascination with judicial definitions. Since our legal documents define the situation as separation and since our courts of necessity treat this definition as not only a normative but also a realistic interpretation of the social facts, our thinking turns around this concept like a fly around a candle. But the judicial definition of the situation will help us as little in understanding it as the judicial definition of a corporation as a person will help us understand the nature of that complex economic institution. Nor will a student of the sexual mores of Americans find much help in trying to understand these if he turns for guidance to the judicial concepts embodied in our statutes on sexual matters. In such cases sociological understanding must be preceded by a mental emancipation from legalistic thought. It is ironical, incidentally, that lawyers can do this more easily than many other people: dealing with the law every day, they have a much better chance of seeing through its fictitious aspects.

These comments are not intended to convey the idea that there is no social reality whatever behind the judicial definition of the situation. There is. But we need concepts other than judicial ones to understand it. Properly applied, a sociological perspective can give us such concepts. In discussing the matter, therefore, we shall once more argue in a sociological frame of reference.

A sociological understanding of the situation could be formulated by saying that the American state is, indeed, separated from any one religious body, but that it is emphatically *not* separated from religion in general.[2] A more colorful way of saying the same thing would be to use a picture from a different area of life. The judicial definition implies the existence of a divorce. The sociological perspective rather suggests a polygamous arrangement in which all wives share equally in the favors dispensed by the husband-state and in which there are careful rules to prevent any one wife from acquiring a position of special privilege. If there is anything at all to the famous "wall of separation," it is a device of judicial architecture to ensure equal access to the royal chamber for all the inmates of this political harem. Possibly it keeps out certain of the less respectable candidates. And (what is perhaps most important) it separates from respectability those few belligerent secularists in our midst who would have nothing to do with this religious-political marriage at all.

The American relationship between religion and politics can be seen more clearly by comparing it with other situations defined judicially in terms of separation. France since 1905 is probably the classical case of this. When the French speak of their republic as being *laique* (a word for which, significantly, there is no adequate English translation), they mean separation not only in our sense of a religious anti-trust act but also in the full sense of the state's being separated from religion in any form. Of course, there are very good historical reasons for this difference, in the anti-clerical tradition of French republicanism on one hand and in the Puritan origins of American democracy on the other. But we are not concerned here with historical explanations. Nor would we prejudice the question as to whether the American arrangement is to be preferred to the French. Our point is simply that the term "separation" means something very different in the two republics and that the American meaning is not adequately represented by its judicial definition.

While the American constitution forbids the establishment of any one religious group in a position of favor in the political order, this prohibition has never seriously threatened the crucial assertion of the American political myth that the foundation of American society is religious. From the beginnings of the country, there has been what Daniel Boorstin has called a "mingling of political and religious thought."[3] Very probably the origin of this is to be sought in the Puritan idea of the "covenant." But, beginning with the modification of this idea in the "halfway covenant" of 1622, the way was opened to a generalization of the idea beyond the narrow confines of the Calvinist fellowship. Despite the gradual erosion of specifically Calvinist contents, what remained was the firm conviction that the American political order was essentially a religious compact. "Americanism," as the vague creed which is supposed to underlie the political order, is explicitly conceived of as a religious attitude. Thus, our political life continues to be infused with religious symbols, religious rhetoric, and religious functionaries. We would contend that this constitutes a *de facto* political establishment of religion, the understanding of which is essential for a clear perception of the situation of the churches in America.[4]

The manifestations of this are so common that it may seem platitudinous to recount them, but often it is the very platitude of a social phenomenon that prevents our perceiving it clearly. It may be worth while, then, to look briefly at these everyday occurrences. There are few political campaigners in this country who will not shroud their appeal in religious language. And there are probably none today who cannot claim some religious affiliation. Politicians in smoke-filled rooms may debate the wisdom of running a Protestant, a Catholic, or a Jew for some particular office—but everyone knows that the avowed agnostic or atheist is not even in the running. Religious affirmations of the "In God We Trust" variety are printed on our currency and our postage stamps. We proudly point to our religion in comparing our political order with the rest of the world—especially its Marxist part, which we habitually describe as the realm of "godless materialism," as if that added the final horror to all the other vices of the Communists. Political events in our country, such as party conventions or legislative sessions or the inaugurations of political executives, are opened with solemn religious ceremonials. The state provides religious functionaries in both its civil and military institutions. And some time ago the federal agency concerned with civil defense inaugurated a special religious program, which, true enough, took cognizance of the practical fact that churches would be handy buildings to use for civil-defense purposes in an emergency, but which also emphasized the role of the clergy in the "spiritual mobilization" of the country in case of war.

But the political establishment of religion means more than moral support. Just as in the establishments of the Old World, it means economic support as well. This writer has always been moved to irony when American Protestants visit Europe and express shock at the state-collected "church taxes" that still exist in some European countries. While it would be rather difficult to work this out in dollars-and-cents detail, the writer strongly suspects that the American state, by virtue of our tax-exemption laws, gives more economic support to the churches than European states in which religious establishments are still legally recognized. American religious groups hold enormous properties in real estate and buildings—all supported by the taxpayers—and the tax-free property is often used as the basis for large-scale investment and capitalization in the secular economy. There is hardly a major denomination in the country today which does not possess an investment commission or agency. If it is argued that this is not really state support because it happens indirectly by the state's refraining from taxation rather than by its directly channeling money to the churches, we would gently suggest that this argument is a sophism. It will, of course, also be argued that the state here is simply treating the churches as it does other nonprofit institutions conducive to the general welfare. We are not concerned here with taking issue with this argument. However, we would contend that the very fact that the religious ritual going on in, say, a tax-exempt Baptist church is deemed to be part of the general welfare just as much as the activities of, say, an institution for the blind is itself evidence of the establishment we are describing. In view of these economic facts, a special irony attaches to recent Protestant outcries against Catholic attempts to milk the public treasuries a little beyond the point which everybody takes for granted. If we may allow ourselves a somewhat crude metaphor here, this is a case of people dwelling in tax-exempt parsonages throwing rocks at those traveling in tax-exempt parochial-school buses. It becomes especially ironical when we reflect that the clerical individuals who cry out against such use of tax money are often the only individuals in the community who themselves do not have to pay property taxes. Since tax funds are not involved, it is perhaps not necessary for us to ask by what rationale these same individuals travel with special reduced-fare tickets on public means of transportation. It would, however, be relevant to raise a further question about the way in which the doctrine of separation relates to the fact that our clergymen constitute the only group of healthy young men with the privilege of a blanket exemption from compulsory military service. Any young American who has had his career interrupted by a letter from his draft board knows that this question has its economic aspect, too.

It is relatively easy to understand the religious content of an establishment such as that of the Church of England or the Lutheran Church of Sweden. It seems more difficult to do so in America. However, the difficulty disappears when we reflect on the cultural religion discussed in the preceding chapter. It is precisely this "common faith" which constitutes the religious content of our establishment. President Eisenhower has supplied us with what may well become *loci classici* of our political religion. For example: "Our government makes no sense unless it is founded in a deeply felt religious faith—and I don't care what it is."[5] Or even better: "I am the most intensely religious man I know. That doesn't mean that I adhere to any sect. A democracy cannot exist without a religious base. I believe in democracy."[6] The closest we get to content is in a statement such as the following: "This is the faith that teaches us all that we are children of God."[7] Or in this most succinct statement: "America is great because she is good."[8] If we combine these definitions of our political religion with what we said previously about our religious-secular continuum, we arrive at some fairly simply propositions: American society possesses a cultural religion that is vaguely derived from the Judaeo-Christian tradition and that contains the values generally held by most Americans. The cultural religion gives solemn ratification to these values. The cultural religion is politically established on all levels of government, receiving from the state both moral and economic support. The religious denominations, whatever else they may believe or practice, are carriers of this cultural religion. Affiliation with a religious denomination thus becomes *ipso facto* an act of allegiance to the common political creed. Disaffiliation, in turn, renders an individual not only religiously but also politically suspect.

The legal disabilities that disaffiliation may still bring about are a good illustration of the nature of our establishment.[9] Avowed unbelievers are not only socially debarred from running for office but also, in some states, may be legally debarred from holding such offices as that of notary public. In some places in this country it is impossible to be married except in a religious ceremony. In many states it is virtually impossible for a childless couple to adopt a child unless they afford proof of church membership. Postwar legislation on the entry of refugees into the country gave to religious agencies the power not only to select the candidates for immigration but also to screen them before their admission and to be responsible for them after it. While it might be argued that these examples affect only relatively small numbers of people, they still illustrate sharply the way in which the religious establishment is on occasion maintained by the direct application of state power. At the time of writing, a case is pending before the Supreme Court to test a Maryland statute under which an avowed unbeliever was debarred from becoming a notary public in that state. The decision is likely to be very significant in terms of the future of the establishment we are discussing. A decision against the Maryland statute would be a large step towards a judicial definition of separation closer to the French concept and further away from the traditional American one.

Various legal controversies surrounding the relationship of religion and the public schools afford us good examples of the nature of the establishment. The Zorach decision of 1952, in which the Supreme Court upheld the release-time arrangements in the public schools of New York state, is a good case in point. The following is from the majority opinion written by Justice Douglas:

We are a religious people whose institutions presuppose a Supreme Being. . . . We sponsor an attitude on the part of government that shows no partiality to any one group and that lets each flourish according to the zeal of its adherents and the appeal of its dogma. When the state encourages religious instruction or co-operates with religious authorities . . . it follows the best of our traditions. For it then respects the religious nature of our people and accommodates the public service to their spiritual needs.[10]

A good example of the confusion surrounding this topic is the recent controversy in Connecticut over transportation of pupils in Catholic parochial schools in tax-supported buses.[11] Here, of course, the subject of controversy was the giving of public funds to one religious group for operations which the other religious groups (not having parochial schools) did not engage in. Without wishing to enter into the particular issue, we would maintain that the crucial fact of the situation was left out of sight entirely— namely, that the public schools themselves engage in religious instruction.

Indeed, a good case could be made for seeing in the public schools the principal agency in our society representing our politically established cultural religion in almost pure form. What is more, as any element of "sectarian" religion is increasingly removed from the curriculum by court actions or merely by social pressures, the cultural religion appears in ever clearer form. This fact has actually made its appearance in some Catholics' defense of their position on parochial schools. Catholics will argue that the public schools do, in fact, teach religious ideas and that these ideas are at variance with the Catholic faith. We would agree with them here. They may also argue that these religious ideas are essentially Protestant, with which argument we would disagree unless one is speaking here of the vaguest historical lineage. Actually, the public schools teach the religious ideas that are embodied in the political order. American values and American democracy take on the nature of a religious cult here. Civics classes expound the beliefs of the cultural religion, perhaps caught most aptly in the often repeated phrase "the brotherhood of man under the fatherhood of God" (which has the interesting implication that brotherhood without this religious foundation is impossible—an unfortunate piece of news for the children of the religiously unaffiliated attending these schools). The ritual aspect of this religious instruction is easily located in the ceremonies of saluting the flag, the reciting of the oath of allegiance in its new explicitly religious form, and other religious-patriotic ceremonies. As in other matters, those religious groups in America that have maintained a degree of tension with the general culture serve to illuminate the situation. Thus, Catholics have helped to clarify the dogmatic contents present in public-school education and Jehovah's Witnesses, who look upon the saluting of the flag as a religious act and do not allow their children to participate in it (in which position the Supreme Court upheld them), have helped to point out the ritual that invariably goes with dogmatic contents.

The relationship of the public schools to our religious establishment has been well stated by Luther Weigle, former dean of Yale Divinity School (who would hardly agree, of course, with our interpretation of his statement):

There is nothing in the status of the public school as an institution of the state, therefore, to render it godless. There is nothing in the principle of religious freedom or the separation of church and state to hinder the school's acknowledgement of the power and goodness of God. The common religious faith of the American people, as distinguished from the sectarian forms in which it is organized, may rightfully be assumed and find appropriate expression in the life and work of the public schools.[12]

If one is to look for a catechism that states these religious suppositions of the public school, John Dewey's A Common Faith will probably be the best choice. This catechism may also be found in the following words of Horace Kallen, certain to be met with enthusiastic approval by the best of our public educators: "For the communicants of the democratic faith it is the religion of and for religions. . . (It is) the religion of religions, all may freely come together in it."[13] And so they do, in the public schools as in our political gatherings. Two groups, of course, are left out of this togetherness of democratic communicants—on the one hand, those who feel an exclusive and perhaps un-American loyalty to only one of the "sectarian forms" (to use Dean Weigle's term), and, on the other hand, those recalcitrant few who find religion in *any* form not to their taste. There may be cause for reflection in this common fate of religious commitment and rejection of religion vis-à-vis the all-embracing cultural religion of our society.

If the public schools offer one good example of our establishment, another good example may be found in the American military chaplaincy.[14] The American military, of course, gives officer's commissions to clergymen of all major religious groups. And, of course, the congregations of these clergymen are made up of soldiers who voluntarily attend the services of their choice (though a sort of "release-time" arrangement may occasionally help to boost attendance). This much is of little interest for our thesis. But, in addition to these "sectarian" activities, military chaplains are ordered to engage in "nonsectarian" operations, to which the voluntary principle no longer applies. The military has called this the "character guidance program." On days set aside in the training schedules, all soldiers of a specific unit are compelled to attend a "character guidance" lecture given by a military chaplain. These lectures normally consist of broad moral preachment, in which soldiers are enjoined to lead "clean, healthy" lives. It goes without saying that patriotism, obedience to military superiors, and zeal in the carrying out of military tasks is part of the morality enjoined. This work of the chaplain is aptly regarded as a "morale factor" by the military. In other words, the religious functionary here performs the shamanic role par excellence—the religious indoctrination of the tribe's warriors as they go out to face the enemy. In a recent study of military chaplains in this country, 79 per cent of the chaplains interviewed thought that "a man with good religious training would make a better soldier than one who lacked such training." In addition, 45 per cent believed that "the killing of an enemy soldier was a righteous act" and the remaining 55 per cent called such killing a "justifiable act."[15] It is not surprising that even hard-bitten martial cynics will look with benign approval upon the activities of these gentlemen. At this point our establishment consists of an age-old religious practice—the consecration of weapons and of those who will use them.

In discussing the American religious situation, Boorstin quotes a passage from Gibbon's *Decline and Fall of the Roman Empire*, pointing out the similarity between our society and that of Imperial Rome:

The various modes of worship which prevailed in the Roman world were all considered by the people as equally true; by the philosopher as equally false; and by the magistrate as equally useful. And thus toleration produced not only mutual indulgence, but even religious concord.[16]

The analogy goes far indeed. In both cases we find a strikingly similar religious picture—many denominations existing together in what Kallen has called a "pluralistic society," tolerating each other with considerable generosity, and with a political cult overarching them all. If the Roman illustration may seem a little too remote in time, the relationship of the Imperial Shinto with the Shinto sects and all other religious groups in pre-MacArthur Japan gives us another very similar picture. One common misconception about early church history is of relevance here. It is commonly thought that the early Christians were persecuted by the Roman authorities because of religious intolerance on the part of the latter. But nothing could be farther from the truth. The crime of the Christians was a political not a religious one. The Roman authorities were completely indifferent to anyone's religious views or practices—as long as these did not constitute a denial of the Imperial cult. Christians hauled before the Roman tribunals during the great persecutions were not asked to renounce any religious views or to affirm others. All that was required for immediate absolution was the putting in evidence of the receipts which certified that the possessor had sacrificed before the Imperial altars. If that were done, the Roman subject holding a Christian "religious preference" might happily go on believing anything he wished or engaging in any ritual of his pleasure. It is interesting to reflect on the fact that the Roman Christians chose martyrdom over participation in this act of political allegiance. Japanese Christians in our own time, after much soul-searching, chose the opposite alternative, deciding that participation in the Imperial Shinto cult was a purely secular act that did not deny their religious faith. The interesting thing about our own Imperial cult is not that Christians participate in it. We would leave open the possibility that a convincing case might be made for this from a Christian viewpoint. What is interesting is that practically nobody even raises the question. It is taken for granted that the "religion of democracy" and the "sectarian" religious groups can exist together without tension—and by many it is even assumed that the "religion of democracy" is the essential core that is the most important common possession of all the denominations.

Tolerance, among both Romans and Americans, is an important aspect of this state of affairs. It becomes much more than a principle of pragmatic mutual accommodation. Tolerance actually becomes a central part of the cultural religion itself. It means not only that everyone has the right to his own religious views but also that he should keep quiet about any strong ones that he may have and certainly that he should refrain from trying to propagate them. But this principle of tolerance applies only to "sectarian" religion. The "religion of democracy" does not have to be tolerant because, by definition, everyone shares in it already. Those radical unbelievers who reject the basic principles of the society (be their rebellion political, social, or moral) have no claim to tolerance. The logic of this is somewhat similar to that under which non-Catholics have been suppressed in Franco's Spain: since all Spaniards are, by definition, Catholic, it makes no sense to talk about the rights of a non-Catholic minority. In this way, under the guise of an all-embracing tolerance, our "religion of democracy" carries within it the seeds of the most unbending intolerance. The McCarthy era has given us a happily brief but nonetheless profound taste of what this can mean.

As has already been remarked, there is a very general lack of insight into these realities within our churches, especially the

Protestant ones. Political reality is perceived through the perspectives of political myth. Kenneth Underwood has stated this
political imperception very clearly in his searching sociological
study of religion in a New England community:

The religious leaders of Paper City are more concerned with the politics
of morality than with the morality of politics. Their discussion of politics
is more largely a way of corroborating their own or their church's
doctrinal and ethical system than an attempt to discover the actual
situations confronting men in the formation of public policy. Most of
the religious leaders believe that their Christian faith and philosophy of
life have given them a system of religious truth and moral principle
with which they may proceed to interpret politics.[17]

We have already seen how much of this "moral principle" is
to be located socially in the Protestant case. As to the "politics
of morality" that Underwood mentions, this is very often to im-
pose the cultural religion of yesterday on the religious establishment of today. Only, rarely is the establishment itself put into
question.

While the basic relationship between religion and politics is
considered to be "given," as Boorstin puts it, the attempt is made
by both major confessions to utilize the establishment in such a
way as will employ the powers of government to enforce what
the religious group considers to be universally binding ethical
norms. Again, it is very ironical when Protestants accuse Catholics
of doing this, innocently unaware of identical procedures within
their own camp. Thus, Catholics are accused of trying to use
governmental power to coerce the general population in the matter of birth control. It is pointed out by Protestant critics that
Catholics are here trying to use the state to enforce a moral
principle that is held only by Catholics and that Catholics want
to compel others to adhere to it. Without making any value
judgment on the issue concerned, we would agree that this criticism is factually correct. What we have here is precisely the same
process as that by which Protestants seek to have the state enforce their own moral principles concerning gambling—which

principles, of course, are not held by Catholics and a good many other people as well. On the whole, simply in terms of the statistics of the situation, Protestants have done much more along these lines in America than Catholics. In fact, as Catholics will point out, even the birth-control statutes in states like Connecticut were originally enacted by Protestants seeking to force their own moral principles of that time on any and all of their less upright fellow citizens. The prime example of this kind of "politics of morality" is prohibition—not only the national disaster of that name, but also the many state and local statutes, still in existence, prohibiting the demon of rum. Legislation in the sexual area (for instance, divorce laws or fornication statutes) would offer us other choice examples of this attempt to utilize the establishment by both major confessions. Despite a rich variety in the alleged moral principles involved in these cases, they have one thing in common—their social and political irrelevance. In practically all these moral crusades, what is at issue is matters of private morality with which the churches, with assistance from the government, want to meddle. The attempts will fail or succeed depending on the particular political constellation of the moment. But only in rare cases will these crusades touch upon matters that seriously concern the large institutions of society. They threaten no vested interest and upset no major applecart. It is a matter of preventing a neighbor from taking a legal drink, or of peeking under his bed for evidence of sexual misbehavior, or of preventing him from spending his money on horses when it could be spent on General Motors common. What is assumed in all these enterprises is the obligation of the state to come to the assistance of the morality enjoined with all the cops at its command—which, after all, may be its share of the bargain in this peculiarly American marriage of throne and altar.

The political religion here discussed is part and parcel of the function of symbolic integration discussed in the last chapter. But in some of the examples we have touched on in the preceding paragraphs an additional function is involved—the one which sociologists call social control. It, too, is a classical social function of religion. Social control is the sum total of coercive means available to a society to bring recalcitrant individuals or groups into line. It may range from capital punishment to the coercive force of gossip. Religion in itself is commonly an agency of social control, internalizing within the individual the norms of society, providing him with psychological mechanisms of guilt and repentance which enable society to get along with a minimal apparatus of external controls. Since our cultural religion ratifies and sanctions the general value system, it naturally has this function within itself as well. But it goes further than this. It reinforces and supports the coercive machinery of the state itself and, in turn, for specific ends, seeks to use this machinery for its own purposes. To put this in a graphic picture—the same government budget that builds the walls of penitentiaries provides the salary of the prison chaplain. And, as any convict will tell you, the clergy are normally on the side of the cops—at least those of our middle-class Protestant churches. In this taken-for-granted alliance between the rectitude of the parson and the policeman lies another clue to the nature of our establishment.

5

Social Religion

Thus far, our sociological analysis of religion in the American situation has been concerned with two basic functions—namely, the functions of symbolic integration and social control. Religion serves to maintain the social structure by integrating and sanctifying the commonly held values on which that structure rests. Already in this function of symbolic integration there is an aspect of what sociologists call social control, since the internalization of controlling values economizes the application of external controls. Or, to return to a simpler picture, religion helps in producing the sort of conscience which allows the society to get along with a minimum of policemen, since the values of the conscience and those of the police force are in general agreement. However, because of its peculiar relationship to the American political order, religion serves even more directly than this as an agency of social control. It is this latter function which we looked at under the heading of political religion. Now it is worth pointing out that, with respect to these two functions, the American situation is far from unusual. Symbolic integration and social control have been time-honored functions of religion in the most varied of cultures, both primitive and advanced, both in the West and in other parts of the world. Indeed, a Durkheimian sociologist would maintain that religion *always* serves to symbolically integrate society and a Marxist would argue that religion *always* constitutes part of the apparatus of social control. To repeat, the writer of this essay would strongly dissociate himself from either "always." He would emphasize that *sometimes* religion serves to disintegrate the social symbols and that *sometimes* religion is downright subversive of the political order. This non-Durkheimian, non-Marxist disclaimer does not change the fact that the two functions occur frequently and cross-culturally. Having come so far, we must now look at a third function of religion in our situation which, if it is not altogether unique, is at any rate peculiarly American in a way in which the other two are not. This is the function of status symbolism.

Today there is much discussion in the American churches of the question of racial segregation. It is frequently pointed out that the churches are still among the most rigidly segregated institutions, and not only in the South. It is often remarked that eleven o'clock on Sunday morning marks the beginning of the most segregated hour in America. And it must be pointed out in fairness that this fact troubles the conscience of many American Christians, and not only in the north. We would contend, however, that the entire discussion of racial segregation and integration in the churches is taking place in a sociological never-never land unless it faces up to a far more fundamental fact of our religious life—that of class segregation. It is not only whites and Negroes who are segregated from each other in their religious activities. Within both racial camps there are clear and often

insurmountable barriers between the churches attended by different socioeconomic classes. True, this class segregation is less visible and often less rigid than the segregation of races. But it is a
reality no less. And, since our society is basically a class society
rather than one constituted by racial castes, this class segregation
is the more fundamental reality to perceive. We may remark in
passing that often the propaganda for racial integration in the
churches and elsewhere inadvertently strengthens this class segregation. Nice Protestant middle-class people of the white race are
assured that the Negroes who want to move into their neighborhood and possibly to join their churches are just as nice and
Protestant and middle-class as they are themselves. By implication, those who do *not* belong in the neighborhood or the church
in question are those, be they white or Negro, who do not fit
into this middle-class constellation of values and mores. In other
words, what goes under the name of racial integration is often
nothing but class integration across color lines.

Once more what we are talking about here is anything but a
mysterious and sinister phenomenon visible only to the morose
imagination of sociologists. We are talking about common and
generally known realities of everyday life in our society. Thus,
a newcomer to an American community is not only asked which
church he intends to join. He is also given liberal advice and
information to help him in the process of choosing. Often enough,
this information is detailed enough to give him a good idea of
the status system of the community in question. Thus, he may
soon discover that Holy Trinity Episcopal and First Congregational are *the* churches in the community, that young executives
and their families feel more at home at the suburban affiliates
of these two churches, that a rather swift crowd has just started
a new Presbyterian church out in Shady Glen, that the Methodist
church in the same area is trying hard but has not quite made it
yet, and so on. We are all familiar with the young Baptist sales-
man who becomes an Episcopalian sales executive. And we have
come across the young couple of Swedish-Lutheran extraction
who would really like to join the Episcopal church but have come

to the conclusion that this would be pushing it socially and settle for Presbyterianism instead. At least within the Protestant camp (the Catholic and Jewish situation is different) these are such commonplace events that they form part of the taken-for-granted reality of existence in society. They do not, needless to say, figure in the official ideology of the churches. Ministers may be the one important group that habitually denies the reality of these events—for obvious reasons, since they contradict sharply the professional self-image and self-conception that ministers aspire towards. Even in this group, however, just a little probing will normally elicit facts which, however obliquely they may be interpreted, are part of this same social reality.

Thus, in America one faces the somewhat strange fact that a person's religious affiliation immediately gives one an idea of that person's social status. True, there are regional and local variations. It is "better" to be a Baptist in Georgia than in Connecticut and "less good" to be a Unitarian in Illinois than in Massachusetts. Also, if one does not know the community in question, one may have to be told that Holy Trinity Episcopal has a status very different from the assemblage of Episcopalians that meets at St. John's five blocks to the south of it. Once these things have been explained, however, religious membership offers a fairly good clue in the sizing up of a person's position in the community. To put this very simply—religious affiliation functions as an indicator of class. But it is not an absolutely accurate indicator. There are some very junior executives at Holy Trinity and even one single Negro Pullman car porter, the pride of the rector's eyes and the man mentioned regularly when the status of the church is officially denied. There are also a couple of erratic corporation vice-presidents at St. John's. By and large, nevertheless, the indicator will work—about as well as any such indicators work in our society. Another way of saying this is that the indicator is a statistical one. When we say that Frenchmen gesticulate when they speak and that Englishmen do not, we obviously do not mean that *every* Frenchman does so and *no* Englishman does. We are simply saying that the probability of finding gesticulating people is much higher in a sample of Frenchmen as against one of Englishmen. It is in the same statistical sense that we are entitled to speak of class churches. Also, while some of these class differences can be understood only after one has learned about the local situation, there are some that are general throughout the society. Thus, one can at least make an intelligent guess anywhere about the respective social status of a Congregationalist or a member of the Church of the Nazarene. If, then, one also knows something about the community in question, the statistical chance of its being a correct guess goes up considerably.

Once more we are not primarily interested here in the historical explanation of how this state of affairs came about. We would point once more to the searching interpretation of the phenomenon in the work of Max Weber.[1] In the opinion of this writer, Weber makes an excellent case in arguing that the situation may be explained historically by a combination of two religious facts—the Puritan ethic, with its strong emphasis on economic rectitude, and the free-church principle, according to which good standing in the church hinged on the individual's living up to these economic values—with a social fact going back to the frontier phase of American society—namely, the need to have some easily recognizable signs to the effect that an individual was good for credit. Thus, as Weber shows in various illustrations, church membership proclaimed the individual's economic reliability. It is clear that this function no longer holds in the same way. What is especially important, as Weber himself pointed out, is that in later American society church membership has come to serve the purpose of social identification along with membership in a variety of other voluntary associations, most of them quite secular in character. Thus, membership in voluntary associations provides a *combination* of indices by which an individual's position may be "plotted," as it were. One may think here, for instance, of a combination of membership in Holy Trinity Episcopal church, the country club, and the board of trustees of the local college, or of membership in the Second Methodist Church, the Elks, and the volunteer fire brigade.

Such indicators of position are very much needed in a society in which people move a lot, both socially and geographically.[2] Especially in the middle strata, one's position is never quite secure. Often it is a very recent achievement. It is then very important to have what Max Lerner has aptly called "badges of belonging."[3] Material possessions and styles of life are helpful to meet this need. Thorstein Veblen's caustic phrase "conspicuous consumption" has served to describe this phenomenon in common American parlance as well as in American sociology. But membership in voluntary associations can be "consumption" in just the same way. At the risk of sounding offensive, we should thus say that there are upper-strata individuals who "consume," say, Congregationalism in the same way and for the same reason that they "consume" *filet mignons,* tailored suits, and winter vacations in the Caribbean. All these elements of consumption indicate to the world (and perhaps to themselves as well) that these individuals have attained a position in society where such things belong. Since, as we have seen, the values within the churches generally reflect those to be found in the individual's milieu in general, there is little to prevent the denominational system from fulfilling this need of our mobile class society. We might point to Robert Lee's recent study of the sociology of the ecumenical movement in America for substantiation of the fact that interdenominational mergers and co-operation commonly occur *within* class lines, thus reinforcing the function just described.[4] The similarity to the case of racial integration mentioned above is telling. Groups of similar class position reach out towards each other across the creedal or racial lines which formerly divided them—and which are significantly alien to the logic of the class system.

While we may be formulating our argument somewhat more sharply than is customary among our usually more soft-spoken sociological colleagues, there is nothing new in the picture we are drawing. The classical statement of the relationship between denominationalism and the class system was made by Richard Niebuhr as long ago as 1929,[5] and nothing that has been discovered since significantly alters his trenchant analysis. As to the function of voluntary associations in indicating status, it was discussed by Veblen over fifty years ago and became a commonplace of American sociology with the detailed studies of the class system inaugurated by the so-called Warner school in the 1940s.[6] The class segregation within American Protestant churches has been uncovered with almost monotonous regularity by one community study after another. Nevertheless, in view of the denial of these facts that one still encounters by spokesmen of the churches, we may be justified in taking a closer look at some illustrations of these findings.

One of the best-known of these studies is Liston Pope's investigation of the relationship of religion and class in a mill town of North Carolina.[7] Distinguishing between three types of churches in the county he studied (rural, mill, and uptown churches—the latter two neatly reflecting the class divisions of the urban community), Pope had this to say about the way these types related to the social reality and the social myth of the situation:

Religious ideals in Gaston County do not approve the recognition of class lines within the churches. One minister affirmed: "If we don't get all these social classes together in the church, I don't know how they ever will be brought together. So I try to make no difference as between uptown folks and mill folks." Despite all such sentiments, the churches have adapted neatly to class segregation. Individual churches, when judged by the type of membership attending, have been almost exclusively either rural, mill or uptown in type.[8]

Pope also underlines the statistical character of this class pattern. There is a small measure of mixing of the classes within the churches. Yet generally any one church has an overwhelming majority of one class in its membership. The way in which the churches related to the coming of the textile industry into the area is also instructive in terms of class dynamics. From the beginning of industrialization, the churches favored the interests of the mills. Churches for the millworkers, increasingly segregated from the older middle-class churches, were developed with the active help of the mill management. It is hardly unfair to use our term of social control with reference to the motives behind this support. In Pope's study the class character of the churches is dramatically illustrated by their reaction to a situation of acute industrial conflict in the community. It is not surprising that this reaction followed closely the class lines dividing the religious institution:

Ministers, individually and in small informal groups, did participate directly, through word and deed, in the crisis. The line of division between Gastonia ministers who in some way opposed and those who in some way countenanced the Loray strike is simple of definition. Salaried ministers of "respectable" churches, with assured status in the prevailing culture, universally opposed the strike; a few ministers of the newer sects and a few lay preachers and ministers without churches supported the strike.[9]

It is only fair to point out that Pope's findings may be connected with the date (1929) and the regional location of this particular strike. It may be doubted whether today, at least outside the South, middle-class churches would take similar action on the side of management in a comparable case. More likely the reaction would be one of indifference and, in the case of the ministers, of ignorance concerning the basic facts in the dispute. But our concern at the moment is not the relationship of the churches to industrial conflict. Pope's study is still significant for its revealing analysis of the reality of class segregation within the religious institution. In this respect, there has been very little change in the last thirty years. For substantiation we may turn here to a recent study by John Morland of a community very similar to that studied by Pope, also a mill community in the Piedmont section of the Carolinas.[10]

Morland found almost exactly the same division between working-class and middle-class churches that Pope did. As did Pope, Morland found that the former generally exhibited sectarian characteristics. But he went further than Pope in setting up an ordinal scale on which each church may be placed in terms of its status in the community. Going "upwards," the scale contains the following churches: Snake cult, Church of God, Wesleyan Methodist, Cromwell Baptist (a mill-village church), First Baptist (a town church), First Methodist, Presbyterian, and Episcopal.[11] With the last, the prestige pinnacle of the community is reached. Beyond that, if anything, is the choir of angels.

Turning to a study of a midwestern community, which James West called "Plainville," we find an almost identical picture.[12] The scale here looks like this, going "downwards": "Christian Church" (Disciples), Methodist, Baptist, and Church of God (Holiness).[13] In the community, which West's study describes as practically obsessed with class, the lines of segregation between these churches are very strong indeed. Interestingly, the lowest stratum in the community (a sort of subproletariat described locally as the "people who live like animals") is completely unchurched. That is, while the denominational system is organized along class lines, there is a pariah group at the bottom which is not admitted into the system at all. This last is an interesting finding, confirmed by the study of "Springdale" by Vidich and Bensman, to which we referred in an earlier chapter. In "Plainville," as in "Springdale," this lowest group is even excluded from the evangelistic perspective:

Proselytizing activities are never aimed at this group; church programs are not designed to appeal to them and ministers never visit them. . . . The ministers and their laymen are often simply unaware of the existence of the traditionally unchurched. They either do not see the unchurched or they have no desire to pollute the church membership with socially undesirable types.[14]

This exclusion of the lowest stratum is significant, as we shall see a little later in our argument.

Class segregation is not limited to small semirural communities. The same pattern is found in larger industrial centers. A good illustration is the study by Kenneth Underwood of "Paper City," an industrial town in southern New England.[15] It is worth quoting some comments by both Protestants and Catholics recorded by Underwood: "I'd like a home in Holy Cross parish." "Next thing you know they'll be joining the Second Congregational Church." "A man can get ahead—meet a lot of fine people—in our church too. I keep telling people, there is more money here than they will admit" (this from a Protestant minister located in a working-class area). "We have everybody in our church from charwomen to bank presidents" (this almost classical delusive statement from the minister of a Protestant church with only three families of wage workers in it).[16] What is particularly interesting in Underwood's study is the finding that Catholic parishes in "Paper City" are even more rigidly segregated by class than are the Protestant churches. While in the latter case the segregation follows the pattern also to be found in secular voluntary associations, in the Catholic case the segregation actually shows signs of planning, with parish lines drawn carefully to follow the lines of residential class segregation in the community.

The following table gives a good impression of what we called the statistical character of this class segregation, that is, of the fact that the separation of classes is not absolute. It ought to be emphasized, however, that the data in the table are drawn from the denominational membership in four *entire* communities; if there had been a further breakdown of the distribution of classes in the denomination's individual churches within each community, the degree of class segregation would have been much higher. However, the table is instructive in showing how far one can generalize about class segregation even without such a breakdown. The table comes from a study of Methodism undertaken by Frederick Shippey:[17]

	WHITE COLLAR		MANUAL	
Place	Population	Methodists	Population	Methodists
Eastern City	49.0%	64.4%	51.0%	35.6%
Southern City	47.5%	70.6%	52.5%	29.4%
Midwestern City	55.3%	75.9%	44.7%	24.1%
Western City	49.8%	65.7%	50.2%	34.3%

This is how Shippey himself summarizes these findings:

Apparently the denomination is having unequal success in bringing a ministry to the American city. Laborers and other types of manual workers are conspicuously in a minority in Methodism. The white collar worker predominates and serves as the backbone of Methodist work in the city. Not only are clerical and sales workers included in this category but also business men and professionals. This does not mean that artisans and other manual employees are missing from membership but that percentage-wise they comprise a minority.[18]

An interesting question is the place of class segregation in the churches of the new American suburbia. At the time of writing, there is as yet a near-total absence of studies of this. However, in this particular case the findings are highly predictable. Since the suburbs, as has been shown in general studies, are very nearly homogeneous in terms of classes residing in any one area, it seems likely that class segregation in suburban churches will be even greater than elsewhere.

To sum up our discussion, we can say that class segregation exists on two levels. On the first level, the local one, we find high measures of class homogeneity in individual churches. On the second level, looking beyond any one community, it is also possible to characterize entire denominations in terms of class, though not as strongly as on the local level. Thus, we are fully justified in speaking of "middle-class churches" and "working-class churches," terms already used by the Lynds in the "Middletown" studies. The line which separates manual and nonmanual occupations (a line which still is very important in our class system) also separates in terms of church affiliation. The religious institution thus mirrors faithfully the class dynamics of the wider society.

This relationship to class dynamics is particularly well illustrated by sociological analysis of lower-class churches, many of which can be described as sectarian. These are the religious groups which Richard Niebuhr called the "churches of the disinherited" and to which Pope devoted a good deal of attention in his Gastonia study. It is suggestive that, in the latter study, it was only within these churches that there was any support at all for the cause of the strikers. It would be rather easy, then, to interpret the relationship of these lower-class churches with the class system in terms of either social protest or social control. It could be that lower-class religion in America functions in *lieu* of political radicalism to give vent to the dissatisfaction and rebelliousness of the underprivileged groups of the population. But there is very little evidence that would support such an interpretation. On the other hand, it could be that lower-class religion, with its emphasis on emotional worship and interest in an otherwordly future, serves as a safety valve through which pent-up frustration and aggression may be relieved in a manner innocuous to the existing power structure—very much along the lines of Marx's concept of religion as an opiate. For this second interpretation there is considerably more evidence, not only for lower-class whites but also—especially—for the Negro churches.[19] However, we would contend that this interpretation also does not give us an adequate understanding of the functionality in question.

A tentative but highly suggestive alternative interpretation was made a few years ago by Benton Johnson in connection with some findings on the values of Holiness sects.[20] Johnson suggests that "Holiness religion may be a powerful agent in socializing lower-class groups in the values and usages of our predominantly middle-class society."[21] Johnson's careful investigations, conducted in the South and on the West Coast, at this point hardly prove, but strongly suggest, that this interpretation is the most viable advanced so far. Lower-class religion is here directly related to social mobility. The values inculcated by the lower-class churches are conducive to upward movement within the class system. Or, to put it more crudely, religious affiliation in these strata separates those who are on the make socially from those who have resigned themselves to their position. This interpretation also throws new light on the fact, commented upon before, of the unchurched character of the lowest stratum. Affiliation with a working-class church thus becomes the first step in the "right" direction for individuals whose sights are set on the middle-class heaven above them. Johnson's interpretation also gives us a better understanding of the missionary and charitable activities undertaken by middle-class churches in the lower reaches. Organizations such as the Salvation Army now appear as agencies of not only religious conversion but also conversion to middle-class values and styles of life. The convert may, indeed, be "washed in the blood of the Lamb"; sociologically, the more significant fact is that he starts to wash literally. Very much the same can be said of white middle-class "uplift" activities among Negroes. The description of the Y.M.C.A. as the "Yes-Man's Crawling Arena" makes the same interpretation in pungent terms. Insofar as such "uplift" is successful, it alienates individuals from their own lower-class milieu and facilitates their entry into middle-class society (in the case of the Negro, of course, this is still a racially segregated "black *bourgeoisie*," to use Franklin Frazier's term).

This discussion of class adds an important element to our general understanding of American religion. The religious groups have symbolic functions not only for the society as a whole but also for specific groups within that society. The ubiquitous phenomenon of class segregation means that religious life is shot through with class characteristics. Thus, the Protestant churches of the "central core" are overwhelmingly middle-class not only in their membership but also in their cultural tone. Their ethics and aesthetics, not to speak of their politics, faithfully mirror the class prejudices and tastes of their constituency. Occasionally there is some modification of the class patterns in terms of traditional religious values (Johnson has aptly called this a "muting" effect), but this is usually in the nature of what sociologists call "cultural lag." That is, there are residues from the past still lingering on which eventually are adapted to the prevailing mores. The step-by-step accommodation of middle-class Protestantism to the sexual mores of that class is a good case in point. But class characteristics concern manners as much as morals. The costume, speech taboos, and interior decorating regarded as suitable for churches offer a rich field for meditation on this subject. The flowered hats, white gloves, and exclamations of "heck" or "darn" become integral parts of a liturgy of gentility. The sociability preferences of the middle class take on religious color. Petty-bourgeois gregariousness is regarded as Christian *koinonia* and the back-yard barbecue takes on the aroma of the *agape* meal in countless church picnics or ladies'-aid gatherings. Needless to say, the details of this religious celebration of class aesthetics will vary with the precise social location in question. Business executives meeting to discuss the finances of Westchester County Episcopalianism will naturally sip their martinis, while Lutheran burghers meeting for their weekly bowling group in some Pennsylvanian town will heartily consume their beer and Southern white-collar wage earners getting together in their capacity of Baptist deacons will partake of wholesome fruit-juice concoctions. What they all have in common is the ready identification of class mores with religious proprieties. Social religion appears here in pure form.

Class segregation and social religion, as described above, has meant a peculiar affinity to the business community for the churches of the "central core."[22] The polity and fiscal structure of these Protestant denominations inevitably brings into positions of lay leadership individuals who are also successful in the economic world. Ministers trained in theological institutions whose outlook may be more "liberal" on social issues commonly find themselves at loggerheads with the lay leaders in their own congregations. Since "success" in a Protestant ministerial career is closely related to the ability to be popular with the laity, it should not surprise us that the pressures from the congregation are generally stronger than the deviant views held by the minister when he left seminary. Some of the generalizations stated as "tentative hypotheses" in a recent study of the churches in the Little Rock crisis bear quoting here:

With an increase in the number of years that the minister has served his congregation, there is a decrease in the probability that he will support desegregation during a crisis. . . .

The minister's support of desegregation is less if his church is engaged in a membership drive, building program, or fund-raising campaign than if it is not so engaged. . . .

Success (speaking numerically and financially) in the ministry is negatively related to the probability of strong advocacy of unpopular moral imperatives during crisis periods. . . .[23]

Substituting "unpopular moral imperatives" for "desegregation" in the first two generalizations as well, we obtain a vivid picture of the price paid by Protestantism for its reliance on lay leadership. It might be added here that only in a minority of cases will these pressures on the minister include direct economic sanctions of the "shut up or get out" variety, although we should not underestimate this possibility. More commonly, however, there are subtler social-psychological pressures at work. Human beings will always tend to adopt the views of the groups with which they normally associate. Since ministers in our "central-core" churches associate primarily with individuals of a certain class position, it is only natural that they will increasingly identify with the class outlook of these individuals. In this way, conflict is avoided and even the possibility of conflict rarely emerges into consciousness. Ministers may then be perfectly sincere when they maintain that they have always acted in accordance with their conscience. The social forces of the situation have already taken care that this conscience will be so formed as to remain innocuous.

Social religion is operative with reference to not only class conflict but also ethnic and racial conflicts. For example, Protestant/Catholic tensions in New England make sense only when one looks at the struggle for political power of the various ethnic groups. Protestant policies on public issues commonly reflect the outlook of the old Yankee segment of the population, driven into a defensive minority status (politically if not economically) by the rise of mainly Catholic ethnic groups, such as the Irish, Italians, Slavs, and French Canadians. Underwood, in the study of "Paper City" mentioned before, gives us a vivid picture of this religious-ethnic conflict. In such situations ethnicity is often a more important factor than class.

The role of the churches in the current integration struggle in the South is a manifestation of social religion in another form. The characteristic posture of the white "central-core" churches is one of passivity, with national or regional denominational gatherings passing resolutions in favor of racial equality—which resolutions are effectively nullified on the local level. But both integrationist and segregationist militancy has its religious support. The new leadership of Negro ministers, freeing themselves from their traditional "Uncle Tom" role and becoming leaders in the integrationist movement, has been commented upon by various observers. At the same time, the white militants in favor of segregation have strong religious leadership as well. There may at first be something bewildering in the spectacle of Negro Baptist ministers acting as N.A.A.C.P. secretaries and white Baptist preachers heading White Citizens Councils. If we understand religion *on both sides* as reflecting the outlook and interests of the respective social constituencies, there will be no more bewilderment. It is important that our sympathies with the Negro cause do not blind us to this important sociological fact. Religion functions in similar fashion, sociologically speaking, when it gives sacred sanction to the integrationist goal as when it identifies the segregationist *status quo* with the divine will. In *both* cases it is operating as social religion in the service of a particular group. It just happens that the interests of one group demand radical change while those of the other call for conservative defensiveness. It also happens that the integrationists have the good fortune of *also* agreeing with the prevailing ethos of the national society. The possibility of specifically religious values, apart from group interests or even opposed to them, is very rarely in evidence in the entire situation. To put this in different words, the phenomenon of, say, the Montgomery bus strike would be evidence against our thesis of social religion only if its leadership came from those *white* groups whose (real or imagined) interests demand the continuation of segregation. There is nothing surprising in the Negro desire to be rid of segregation and to find religious support for this goal. Needless to say, such sober sociological evaluation in no way invalidates the rightness of the Negro cause; it just stops us from seeing in it something that it is not—namely, an emancipation from social religion.

A statement that is sometimes made about Protestantism is that it is the "religion of the *bourgeoisie*." Such a statement need not necessarily be due to Marxist influence. An inadequate understanding of Weber's theory on the relationship of Protestantism and capitalism may also be behind it. Also, the statement offers a facile ordering principle for the puzzling variety of religious-social phenomena in American society. Our analysis would indicate that the statement is a gross oversimplification. Protestantism is not limited in its membership to the middle class, but extends both above and below it. Even the "central-core" denominations, to whom the statement might be applied with greater validity than to Protestantism as a whole, contain many individuals of working-class status. If the statement applies to values rather than to membership, it gains plausibility. The morals, mores, and manners of Protestantism are strongly "bourgeois" in character, at least historically. In the middle classes, as we have seen, the old "Protestant ethic" analyzed by Weber is increasingly being replaced by the more permissive "social ethic" discussed by Whyte. The lower-class churches retain a stronger emphasis on the old "ascetic" values, a fact which is functional in terms of class mobility if we allow the validity of Johnson's interpretation. Neither of the two groups of churches, with the possible exception of upper-class Episcopalianism, retains any vestiges of a nonbourgeois or even an antibourgeois ethos. This much is probably certain. However, if we look at Protestantism as a whole, a more subtle term is called for to describe its social location.

Johnson has suggested a very apt phrase in this connection— the "community of the respectable." True, respectability has a generally middle-class character. But not only middle-class people are respectable. In fact, respectability may be more important in the lower or working classes, because the latter are much closer to the blatantly nonrespectable. Over and beyond the function of class indication, religious affiliation serves as an act of allegiance to this wider community referred to in Johnson's phrase. In this connection, we would recall once more what was said in a previous chapter about the relationship of religion and the secular value system. The act of joining a religious group manifests publicly the adherence to this value system and to the majority of the nation which embraces it. The findings mentioned before on the nonaffiliation of the lowest stratum now obtain an additional meaning. Religion is something for those who have a stake in and a commitment to society as it now exists. Those who are excluded from respectability, be it by their own choice or that of others, are *ipso facto* outside the religious institution which is a pillar of that respectability. This applies not only to those located in "society's basement," to use a term of hobo literature—the "white trash," the dwellers in "shack towns," skid rows, or migrant labor camps. It also applies to other deviants, rebels, and nonconformists. Social religion has little toleration for the intellectual or moral radical, or anyone who flaunts the canons of respectability. Again, as we have seen, respectability does not mean the same thing on different levels of the class system. However, there is sufficient homogeneity of values in American culture at least to draw clearly the limits beyond which respectability is impossible. Religion exists *within* these limits throughout the society.

Robert Lee, to whose study we have already referred, has shown very convincingly how "ecumenicity" in America is related to this coexistence of classes in the "community of respectability." We might add that the whole "interfaith" movement, as illustrated best by the National Conference of Christians and Jews, becomes comprehensible sociologically in the same way. Class segregation continues to be the prevailing pattern within the religious institution, but all classes that belong to the realm of respectability can affirm this allegiance in religious terms. Not only is this "interfaith" solidarity functional in maintaining the social system as it now exists, but it also has an ideological function as well—namely, it serves to obscure the reality of class segregation. Having participated in the rhetorics of tolerance and mutual good will, one may now harbor the illusion that the social divisions of the society have been superseded by religious solidarity. At this point social religion gives birth to social mythology.

6

Psychological Religion

A number of beliefs are very widespread in our churches about the relationship of religion and psychological well-being. These beliefs might be summarized in the following way: Religion is highly beneficial, perhaps even essential, to the psychological integration of the individual. Religion provides meaning and purpose in life. It gives inner strength to cope with both minor and major crises. It alleviates anxiety and makes for a mature approach to one's problems. It helps the individual to relate to others, in the family and beyond. In general, religion is conducive to mental health.

Such beliefs are probably shared by the great majority of the religiously active, but they are frequently brought up as illustrating the desirable consequences of religion even by those who are more distant from the religious institution in their own life.

What is more, these beliefs are used extensively in the promotional activities of the churches (Protestant, Catholic, and Jewish) and of organizations like the Advertising Council, which expends hundreds of thousands of dollars to tell Americans to go to the church of their choice and derive strength for the week ahead. These beliefs are central elements in the ideologies of the religious education movement (which, characteristically, is interfaith in nature) and the various movements that seek to develop psychotherapeutic programs under religious auspices.

We have deliberately formulated these beliefs in their, as it were, minimal form. Anyone familiar with popular religion in America today can easily point to much more comprehensive formulations, in which religion appears in a purely magical way as an instrument for wordly success. The name of Norman Vincent Peale is perhaps sufficient allusion to this constellation.[1] It seems to us that, despite the continuing mass appeal of Dr. Peale's mental alchemy, no useful purpose would be served here by concentrating on this grotesque exaggeration of what is really a much more general phenomenon. We may leave Dr. Peale and his imitators to the ongoing barrage of the neo-orthodox artillery and turn rather to an analysis of the more general phenomenon.

There are various theories explaining the psychology of religion in terms of the individual's need to integrate his life meaningfully and, in the process, to deal with his frustrations and anxieties.[2] It is not our concern in this essay to argue the general merits of these theories, although the writer inclines to the view that religion will at least tend towards such psychological functionality. What is our concern, however, is to point to the psychological dimension of the American religious situation analyzed in the preceding chapters—or, conversely, to suggest that there is a sociological dimension to the psychological beliefs just described. We would contend that the belief (and perhaps the fact) that religion is psychologically functional is itself grounded in the social existence of religion. In other words, there is a psychological side to the religious establishment. This is what we would call psychological religion here.

There are historical situations in which certain religious movements are *not* established socially, in which they may be marginal to society, despised, or even persecuted. The psychologist might find that even in such situations religion might satisfy certain psychological needs, possibly masochistic, self-punishing, or other neurotic needs. This does not interest us here. It is quite clear, however, that whatever the psychological functionality might be in such instances, it will be different from what happens in situations where religion is respected, taken for granted, and frequently associated with social rewards. For example, the psychology of religious martyrdom is very unlikely to be able to use such concepts as "maturity," "mental health," or "social adjustment," which figure prominently in our own psychological religion. Whatever else he may be, the Christian about to be eaten by lions in a Roman arena is hardly showing a very "mature" attitude towards his problems—and he is certainly not "adjusted" to his society.

Our psychologists tell us that the mentally healthy individual is one who is capable of coping with reality. What they commonly overlook is that reality itself is socially constituted. The values and cognitive beliefs of a society construct the world in which its members live. The place of religion in this socially constructed world will determine the way in which it will help or hinder the individual in adjusting to reality. We would then contend, from a purely sociological point of view, that the beliefs described in the opening paragraph of this chapter are appropriate to a situation in which religion is socially embedded in the general value system. In such a situation, religion will indeed tend towards the social adjustment of the individual. It may even assist the individual to be a more successful participant in the society. Since social adjustment generally raises the level of satisfaction, reducing frustrations and anxieties, it is also very likely that religion in this situation is conducive to emotional balance. We are even tempted to the formulation that, to the degree that religion functions in society as an integrative force, it will function to integrate the individual psychologically as well. The findings of social psychology about the "internalization" of the norms of society within the individual would certainly support this formulation. While we cannot claim conclusive proof of our contention, we would argue that there are significant pointers in this direction in the data we have about American religion.

In this social-psychological constellation, religion becomes an essential element of what we might call the "O.K. world." The religious institution becomes to the individual a guarantee that the world is as it should be. Affiliation with the religious institution becomes an act of allegiance to the "O.K. world," to normalcy, to the *status quo.* The frequently observed fact that Americans tend to join churches when they marry or when their children reach Sunday-school age makes sense against this background. The individual feels that he has a stake in the social world. He has sown his proverbial wild oats. The time has come to settle down. The married state and the religious affiliation proclaim together this surrender of the irresponsible freedom of youth. Since the religious institution fosters the values of "responsibility" (that is, of conservative adaptation to the world as socially defined), it becomes a direct help in this process of adjustment. It helps to integrate the individual's intellectual and emotional life in the way required by his "responsible" existence. The success of the institution may be measured by the degree to which its values seem ultimately right and even taken for granted by the individual, so that any discrepancies between values and conduct is blamed not on the institution but on the individual's own foibles. If this measure is used, our religious institution is very successful indeed. And, of course, the institution also provides the psychological mechanisms by which these foibles can be rationalized and atoned. In our Protestant churches a general anthropology of tolerance and renewed effort takes the place here of the Catholic sacramental apparatus. Wherever the individual may find himself at the moment on his moral path, the institution remains as the symbol of the "O.K. world," which is the ultimate criterion of his conduct.

Our term "O.K. world" is excellently illustrated in the classical study of "Middletown." We are quoting here some of the answers of middle-class people to the Lynds' question about what church-going means to them:

I was brought up to go to church and I just feel uneasy as if something is wrong with the day if I don't go. I often get something from church that helps me through the week.

I would hate to live in a community where there was no church. I must confess I am not as interested in church or in church work as a good many. Lots of the time I am just plain bored by church, but I feel I ought to go.

Church going is one thing I insist on with my family. Loyalty to religion is the foundation of all the rest of life and the church is the one institution that represents it.[3]

The same motifs mark the promotional statements used by the churches of "Middletown" to induce people to come to them:

The church is one of the fundamental institutions and should be supported.

Come and join us in our morning services next Sunday. . . . Note how much better you will feel the whole day long.

No city has a more wonderful bunch of churches than has Middletown. Select one and make it your Church—the place where you can worship God, learn of His world program, become associated with the best people, and where you will find a glorious opportunity for service. . . . We can help you in sickness, in sorrow, in trouble. But our greatest blessing for you is simply an opportunity to make your life count big for the uplift of people right here in Middletown and unto the uttermost parts of the world.[4]

If we leave aside the class appeal of associating with "the best people," we have here in a nutshell the psychological functionality we are arguing for—integration of the individual, even in his personal crises, into the ongoing life of the community. As the Lynds themselves sum up their findings on religion in "Middletown":

As in the case of civic loyalty and patriotism, in church question marks straighten out into exclamation points, the baffling day-by-day complexity of things becomes simple, the stubborn world falls into step with man and his aspirations, his individual efforts become significant as part of a larger plan.[5]

Sociological studies of the sensitivity evinced by the Lynds are rare, but we have no reason to believe that the meaning of churchgoing has changed appreciably since then. William Whyte's findings about religion in Park Forest some twenty years after the first "Middletown" study show us a very similar constellation. The following quotation is from Hugo Leinberger, the exchaplain who developed the United Protestant Church in that suburb of Chicago:

I think this is the basic need—the need to belong to a group. You find this fellowship in a church better than anywhere else. And it is contagious. In a community like Park Forest, when young people see how many other people are going to church regularly, they feel they ought to. Another need we fulfill is that of counseling. Young people want a place to take their problems and someone to talk to about them. Put all these things together and you get what we're after—a sense of community. We pick out the more useful parts of the doctrine to that end.[6]

Nor has the promotional line changed much, as the following church advertisement (this one from New York rather than Chicago) quoted by Whyte indicates:

Lots of acquaintances—not many friends. Is this increasingly true for you? Look at your life. You may find that it lacks those spiritual experiences which bring people together in understanding and friendship. Participation in the activities of the neighborhood church supplies the spiritual force to weld lasting friendships. Meet future friends in church next Sunday.[7]

The child-centered character of suburban religiosity has been borne out by other studies.[8] Park Forest itself was the subject of another careful study, this one concerned with the Jewish community there.[9] Striking similarities with Leinberger's pan-Protestant *koinonia* were found. The following are statements by Jewish residents of Park Forest explaining the meaning to them of the establishment there of a Jewish center:

They (the women) hadn't faced Jewish life, they didn't care for Jewish values, but they recognized that they were Jewish and they needed a Sunday school because the kids asked for it. . . . They wanted a non-sectarian Sunday school.

As we train the children, you will have to train them yourself . . . you'll have to move towards a community center and a synagogue eventually . . . and give the children support.

I want him (the child) to have more security and acceptance in regard to his status and relationship with society—be better prepared than I was.

The parents aren't interested but they sort of give their kids Sunday school as a castor oil, a preventative for what ails the parents.[10]

This curious phenomenon of the vicarious religiosity of the child could, of course, be explained in deeper psychological terms—perhaps as a lingering religious dread that expresses itself in superstitious concern for one's children. But we would steer clear of such Freudian (or even Jungian) underbrush. Quite apart from deeper psychological anxieties that may be operative here, such data point up clearly the relationship of religion to what we have called the "O.K. world."

The increasing use of the terminology and techniques of psychotherapy within American Protestantism illustrates from another direction the constellation we seek to describe.[11] Again, it is not necessary for us to look at those aspects of this movement that are a sort of thin Protestantization of Christian Science. Our point is made just as well if we look at the "respectable" elements in the movement. The man-in-the-street opinion that religion is essentially a reservoir of "spiritual forces" to help one live one's everyday life is translated here into more sophisticated language. The religiously more offensive components of the Freudian ideology are purged. The psychologically "positive" aspects of religion are integrated into a psychotherapeutic enterprise which helps individuals to feel more at ease with themselves and with their existence in society. In other words, religion and psychotherapy become allies in the bringing about of emotional stability and social adjustment. Since the psychotherapeutic movement is split into a number of competing denominations, there is a great variety within this less than holy alliance. There are the different organizations seeking to train ministers in psychotherapeutic techniques. There are the attempts to introduce "group dynamics" and "sociodrama" into the program of the churches. There is, above all, that whole movement of building a new profession on "religious education," with an ideology representing a sometimes surrealistic blend of Horace Bushnell, John Dewey, and an emasculated Freud. It is not our purpose here to discuss the merits of any of these enterprises. We would only point out their intimate relationship to the afore-mentioned psychological functionality of religion in our middle-class churches. To repeat our main contention: Religion functions sociologically to represent the integration of the society. Religion may then function psychologically as a "socializing agency," that is, to assist the individual to adjust to this society and to be happy in the process.

Wayne Oates has coined the apt phrase "the cult of reassurance" to describe this religious-psychological complex.[12] Though Oates was referring mainly to Dr. Peale's brand of the commodity, the phrase is descriptive of the much wider phenomenon in which we are interested here. After reviewing various manifestations of this "cult," Pealist and other, Roy Eckardt sums the matter up succinctly in the following words: "For the American citizen, the Protestant, Catholic and Jewish faiths tend to furnish a psychosocial resting place."[13] It may be worth our while to look at some further examples of how the promotional machinery of institutional religion plays on this theme.

Dan Wakefield has written a bitter "content analysis" of a popular Protestant family magazine, *Together,* in which its character is summed up as follows:

It is a peculiar reassurance that popular Christianity seeks to convey to its followers—that its current disciples are so like the man in the street, and so unlike the Savior of the Bible. In expounding this message, the modern churchmen have sought to transform that Savior into the Christ of *Together*—a face indistinguishable from the rest of the lonely crowd. . . . In the desperate effort to be up-to-date, they (the religious leaders) have dressed Jesus Christ in a grey flannel suit and smothered his spirit in the folds of conformity. The new slick-paper Christianity cheerily rises in the midst of a world seeking answers to survival, and offers an All-Methodist football team.[14]

When we look at the details of Wakefield's analysis, we find all the hallmarks of "socializing" that we have just discussed— friendly advice to the readers on "spiritual efficiency," information on members of the magazine's denomination who are engaged in various hobbies, recommendations on motion pictures and books for family consumption, advice on how to handle personal problems in a sensible manner, and so forth.

Another excellent analysis of religious mass communication of this variety is Frederick Elkin's discussion of the motion picture *The Next Voice You Hear.*[15] The motion picture is presented as a modern parable, in which a voice suddenly heard on the radio is identified as that of the divinity. The impact of this supernatural intervention on a typical American family is shown. The "theology" of the motion picture is quite simple, as summarized by Elkin:

God exists and watches over us. . . . We should have faith in Him and not be afraid. . . . If you have faith in God and live according to His word, all will be well in the world. There will be no bitterness between an employer and an employee, between a husband and his in-laws, between a policeman and a citizen, and presumably, between one nation and another. With such faith and a good life, a son will not try to worry his mother, a pregnant woman will bear her child without difficulty, and perhaps even a defective automobile starter will begin to work properly.[16]

The detailed social imagery that appears in this parable is even more instructive than its explicit message. It stresses the "O.K." character of typical middle-class family life, condemning by implication those who reject that life. It suggests the central importance of the woman in the family as wife and mother. It sanctions the values of our economic and political systems, presenting in a religiously favorable light such authority figures as the foreman and the policeman. Social harmony within this *status quo* is the will of the divinity. Social conflict, by implication, is evil.

There is good reason to think that the psychological functions of religion may be somewhat different in the lower-class churches, for reasons that may be implicit in our previous sociological analysis of these groups.[17] What is interesting, however, is the appearance of a very similar religious-psychological constellation in movements with very diverse religious messages. For instance, Moral Re-Armament, with all its pseudorevolutionary fervor, ends up by serving the psychological integration of the individual into our present social system.[18] But a movement as different as the evangelistic crusade of Billy Graham strangely leads to the same result. Here is how two astute sociological observers summarize the appeal of the famous revivalist:

He addresses himself to the respectable pillars of the church and to nominal believers who attend his mass rallies in order to be made "authentic. . . ." The way to *certainty* is presented as easy, and the mass of others who are present makes it even more natural to think of this as the popular and approved and obvious way. Thus, one's beliefs are authenticated without exacting any real price or irrevocable commitment. The sin to be confessed is nominal sin. There is no need to renounce drink, or ambition, or home, or bank account, or smart apparel. . . . And simply by affirming, in public, that they are respectable, believing, upright, moral persons, these decision-makers thus earn the approval of anonymous third persons who, like themselves, wear no crown of thorns but are all for others wearing it. . . . The revival thus offers an opportunity to persons who hold on to outmoded ideals for the expression of inauthentic commitments.[19]

We should be careful at this point not to overstate our case. It should be made clear that we are speaking here of tendencies, not making generalizations that hold absolutely without exceptions. There are certainly individual churches, on various class levels, in which this psychological functionality is modified by the classical Christian emphasis on transcendence and judgment. The influence of the neo-orthodox movement on Protestant preaching and literature in various places is certainly a "countervailing force." So is fundamentalism in certain cases. Catholicism, despite the activities of Bishop Sheen, still stands in massive contradiction of this sort of functionality. Nevertheless, we would abide by the contention that what we have described here as psychological religion is an enormously powerful tendency within middle-class Protestantism (and very probably within middle-class Judaism as well).

If one allows the validity of our contention, one will not be surprised by various findings on the relationship of religion to such social-psychological complexes as "authoritarianism," "ethnocentrism," and "conformity." We are introducing these findings with some hesitation, because there are critical questions that could be raised about the methodology of some of these studies. However, we would still feel that the wide agreement between various such studies concerning the effect of religion is instructive for our purposes.

The classical studies of prejudice by Adorno, Allport, and their associates all point in one direction.[20] They suggest that Americans who maintain some religious affiliation express more racial and ethnic prejudice than those who are not so affiliated. This finding, however, is modified by the further suggestion that this is mainly true of those whose religious affiliation is a conventional matter rather than of those whom Weber would call "religious virtuosi." As Adorno put it:

There is much in the interivew material to support the view . . . that the more religion becomes conventionalized, the more it falls in line with the general outlook of the ethnocentric individual.

The adherent of what Kierkegaard, a hundred years ago, called "official Christianity" is likely to be ethnocentric although the religious organizations with which he is affiliated may be officially opposed to it, whereas the "radical" Christian is prone to think and to act differently.[21]

Allport makes a parallel distinction between what he calls "institutionalized" and "interiorized" religious outlooks.[22] While this distinction affords obvious comforts to those who recoil from the association of religion with prejudice, it is important to keep in mind that the great majority of churchgoers (and, thus, the majority in the samples used in these various studies) fall into the "official/institutionalized" rather than the "radical/interiorized" category. Independent investigations have, on the whole, confirmed Adorno's and Allport's findings.[23]

By far the most telling findings in this area are those of Rose Goldsen and her associates in their recent study of American college students.[24] Using a simple and fairly defensible measure of religiousity, these investigators have come up with very interesting correlations, some of which are the following:

Religious students are more likely to see moral implications in cheating; more likely to feel a norm justifies cheating.

Religious students are more likely than others to express conformity to the prevailing values of their major social role.

Religious believers are more likely than others to agree with the vocabulary of prejudice.

The higher a group's score on the scale of religiousness, the more prevalent in that group is expressed approval of the idea of constraining, say, "people with dangerous social and economic ideas," or those of unproved "loyalty."[25]

The clue to the interpretation of these findings is given in the following passage:

Religious believers seem to feel more integrated in society; non-believers seem more alienated from it. Religious believers tend to testify to the kinds of behavior and belief that conform to the standards of propriety of American culture; non-believers are less likely to do so. Religious believers are more likely to respond to the pressure of a social norm, even on an issue that they regard as a moral question (such as cheating on examinations). Perhaps these are all aspects of conformity to the dominant values of the social groups to which these students belong.[26]

Here we find brought together very clearly both sociological and psychological aspects of the religious-secular continuum of values discussed before in this essay. The religious do not hold values that are significantly different from those of others. But they hold to these values more strongly. Religion provides both social and individual integration of these values. The religious institution serves to "socialize" the individual in such a way that he will conform to the norms of his social group, regardless of what these norms are. Insofar as the norms include prejudice or anti-democratic values, religion serves to accentuate these as well. In lucid form we are confronted here with the psychological dimension of our religious establishment.

We may return here for a moment to our consideration of the nature of American culture in Chapter 3 of this essay. We argued there that this culture is characterized by a concentration on the "daylight" side of life and an avoidance of ecstasy in all its forms. The "O.K. world" discussed in the present chapter is, of course, identical with the cultural constellation described before. The writer of this essay has dealt elsewhere with the possible relationship between religion and what Jean-Paul Sartre has called "bad faith."[27] Suffice it to say here that a religious establishment such as ours is highly conducive to "bad faith," in Sartre's sense. That is, religion provides the individual with the means by which he can hide from himself the true nature of his existence. Religion reassures and strengthens him in his social roles, however "inauthentic" these may be. Religion thus tends to be an obstacle in the progress towards "authenticity" as a person. In a word, religion prevents ecstasy. It prevents the individual from stepping outside the routines of his everyday life in society and looking at himself in freedom. Instead, it ratifies the routines, sanctifies the values by which the social roles are rationalized, comforts the individual if personal crises threaten his social adjustment. The "O.K. world" is the world of "inauthenticity." It should be emphasized that, when we make this statement, we do *not* imply that this world is necessarily bad morally. We are simply saying that the individual is effectively prevented from exercising free choice with regard to this world— a choice which presupposes an experience of ecstasy (in the literal meaning of *ekstasis*—standing outside, stepping outside the routines which society tells us to take for granted). The psychological processes that we have discussed in this chapter provide the effective walls of this imprisonment.

With these considerations we have come to the end of this first, the analytic part of our argument. We began our analysis of religion in American society by pointing to a paradox—the paradox that on the one hand religion must be highly functional in American society and that on the other hand it appears to be irrelevant in terms of the moving forces in this society. We then suggested that an analysis of the religious establishment would provide the clue to the paradox. The reader will have to judge how convincing our argumentation has been. The answer which we would give to our initial question should be clear now. The paradox resolves itself in a simple proposition: *The social irrelevance of the religious establishment is its functionality.*

If organized religion in this society were highly relevant to the major social institutions, it would not be functional in the way it now is. It is functional precisely to the degree in which it is passive rather than active, acted upon rather than acting. It is in this capacity that it is respected socially and supported politically. It is in the same capacity that it meets many important psychological needs of the individual. As we have said a number of times in the preceding pages, we would not insist on the exceptionless validity of this equation between irrelevance and functionality. We would simply maintain that the major social forces in our situation tend towards the repeated realization of the equation. The failure to see this makes impossible any meaningful Christian thinking about the American situation. And, we may add, this failure of perception is itself functional, because it is likely to be part of an optimistic ideology which obscures the real state of affairs.

III

Interlude—Some Counciliatory Comments

Before we proceed to the second, the (hopefully) constructive part of our argument, there are two questions that we ought to linger over for a moment. Both questions concern the analysis we have just undertaken. The first question is this: What has been left out in our analysis? The second question is a little different: Assuming that our analysis is substantially correct, why is there any reason for concern? Or, more simply: So what?

The first of these two questions is easier to answer, if only because the discipline of sociology itself already implies an answer. Yet it is important to deal with the question, if only briefly, because there are certain thoughts that have probably arisen in the mind of the reader. Perhaps these thoughts could be well summarized in the words of Robert Miller, who concludes as follows his careful study of the social attitudes of American Protestantism between the two world wars:

Lastly, one need not be too cynical about the efforts of the churches to achieve a society which approximated a divine ideal. Because the world at mid-century fell terribly short of this absolute mark, it does not follow that the effort should not have been made in the first instance. Every generation must fight the good fight in its own way and in its own day, and count itself lucky if it has inched forward almost imperceptibly toward a more just social order. At mid-century the churches know they cannot expect perfection within history. They know too that corrupt man can do little without the forgiving grace of a sovereign King.

But these truths must not paralyze the social conscience of American Protestantism. It is just possible that America is a little finer because of the activities of the churches. If a righteous God condemns the churches for their abysmal deviations from absolute standards, a fallible historian can yet find much in the social attitudes of the Protestant churches of America, 1919–39, that is hopeful and charitable.[1]

It goes without saying that we have left out very much in our analysis. We have left out a complex intellectual development among the best minds of American Protestantism, a development which represents a steady advance towards greater realism concerning the nature of society. The name of Reinhold Niebuhr may serve as a symbol for this development. We have also left out the frequent attempts of denominational and interdenominational bodies to speak relevantly on specific social issues. These attempts may often have been naïve, but they have almost always been well-intentioned. We have left out the courageous attempts of Protestant ministers and laymen to witness to the social implications of their faith in local situations of crisis or conflict. Finally, we have left out completely the question of what the churches have meant to many individuals in their search for religious truth, beyond and even within the functionalities that we have analyzed.

A critic of our argument might feel that these omissions invalidate the whole analysis. But we are not prepared to accept this criticism. It is true that any effort to understand will abstract from reality, will look at some things and not take others into consideration. This is especially true of the efforts of the sociologist who, unlike the historian, will always tend to look for generalizations, will therefore be inclined to be dissatisfied with the simple accumulation of facts, and will want to see how these facts relate to the ongoing life of the entire society he is studying. The motto of the sociologist is very likely to be *"aude errare sed aude finire"*—that is, have the courage to make mistakes but, above all, have the courage to conclude. There are some, especially historians, who will hold this tendency against the sociologist. We will not enter here into a methodological argument; we will only maintain that in what we have done we have tried to be faithful to an intellectual tradition of which sociology is the product.

If we look specifically at the above-mentioned aspects of the situation left out of our analysis, we can be conciliatory in granting that these aspects exist, but we shall also maintain that their existence does not detract from our argument. If we have left out of our analysis the changes in Protestant theological thought about society, this is because we have tried to undertake a sociological analysis, not to write a history of ideas. The same is true of the omission of pronouncements by various ecclesiastical bodies. In both cases we would contend that there is little evidence that the real (as distinct from the ideal) functionality of religion in American society has been very much affected. For example, the integrationist manifestoes of religious assemblies have rarely resulted in any changes in the local situations to which the delegates have returned after these assemblies. And if the statements on racial segregation have been ineffective, statements on class segregation are rarely heard at all. If we have left out individual exceptions to the trends we have analyzed, this was certainly not in order to depreciate the human and religious values that may be found in these, but simply because they *were* exceptions and as such not very helpful in trying to understand the over-all picture. If, finally, we have not spoken of what may go on in the religious experience of individuals, this is because such experience is by definition beyond empirical analysis. Our analysis could not deal with the presence of God. By its very nature it had to limit itself to the world of men. The sociologist is also in no position to speak of the absence of God. He is in a very good position to speak of the absence of social relevance among those who claim to represent Him. He is also in a position to note when, in the actual testimonies of men, the representation is of the gods of secular society rather than of the God spoken of in the sacred texts.

A final comment to be made about this first question concerns what the American sociologist Robert Merton has aptly called "latent functions." Not all functions in society are "manifest"— that is, conscious, intended, publicly recognized. Indeed, many of the most important functions are, in Merton's sense, "latent" —that is, unconscious, unintended, not part of the generally available consensus of the society. Latent functionality is a concept very close to irony (as, for example, Reinhold Niebuhr has used it in speaking of American history). It reminds us that the real consequences of their actions are often hidden from the actors themselves. It warns us not to be beguiled by what people say, even if we are convinced that they say it with sincerity. We cannot understand the real functionality of an organization by just reading its bylaws. It would be equally naïve to seek an understanding of a complex religious institution by just looking at the explicit social philosophy expounded by its representatives. Inevitably the quest for sociological understanding leads us into the areas of the unsaid and the unrecognized. So much, then, for our first question.

The second question is more difficult to answer because it involves our convictions much more than our methodology. And so, of necessity, this is the point in our argument when the writer must come out of his analytical detachment and be ready to engage his values. Logically the same will be true of the reader.

Our analysis in the preceding part of this essay has tried to demonstrate a certain relationship between religion and society in America. We have argued that this relationship, characterized as a religious establishment, functions in religion to integrate and support society and to adjust the individual to society. It should be obvious that whether or not one finds this relationship alarming will depend on one's view of its two components. That is, our concern in the matter will depend on our view of religion and our view of society—or, rather, of this particular society. And it is certainly possible that there are viewpoints on these which could lead one to shrug one's shoulders, agree with everything, and then say, "So what?" This point calls for further clarification.

If one feels that American society is in itself evil, then certainly everything that serves to perpetuate this society must be evil also. In that case, of course, religion in American society would be morally abhorrent. It would be part and parcel of a social reality to be rejected and condemned. A person believing in some alternative ideal of society (such as Communism) would naturally take this position. But a person comparing social reality with some absolute standard of idealism (such as many pacifists tend to do) might also come close to such a position. American society and American religion might then be bracketed together in a modern version of Voltaire's famous saying about the superstition, intolerance, and fanaticism of the church of his time: *"écrasons l'infâme"*—"let us crush the vile thing." The existential result of an analysis such as ours would then be resistance, revolutionary fervor, or, at the very least, the contempt of inner withdrawal. Our essay would then have to address itself to some sort of intellectual underground. In the absence of a political underground, we might at least find a haven in the subterranean world of beatnik sectarianism or some personally congenial variation of it.

Having no alternative ideal of society to offer and being skeptical of any form of social utopianism, the writer of this essay must reject these intriguing possibilities. We live in a world of relativities. It is within these relativities that our moral and political commitments must be made. American society is neither paradise nor purgatory. History offers us few luxuries and almost never the luxury of living in a golden age. But even within this world of relativities, even if we refuse to look at reality in terms of white and black, there are sharp contrasts. These contrasts make possible our moral choices. The cynical perspective of the world as the night in which all cats are gray is rarely honest. We would contend that it is quite dishonest when we compare our American situation with the contrasting possibilities that our contemporary world has to offer. Political propagandists who hold up the picture of a righteous America confronting a Communist inferno confuse the issues. But so do those who compare us with our international antagonists and wish the plague on both our houses. American society is far from perfect. But its imperfections weigh relatively lightly when we compare them with the total horrors of the most recent history. This is something to repeat often not only to our Marxist critics but also, for example, to many "professional Europeans" or observers in the "uncommitted nations" who refuse to see significant differences between the various choices open to us today. American culture, it is true, has in it aspects that are repulsive and nauseating to the values of many. But it has also forces of creativity, strength, and sheer human decency that compare well with any contemporary society. American democracy may often appear as an incongruous circus of corruption and hypocrisy, as may American capitalism, but then we may suddenly come upon astounding signs of moral commitment within it. And, with all its corruptions, our political and economic system has so far stayed clear of those monstrous terrors that have been the daily fare of those living under totalitarianism. Our very corruptions have commonly been in the nature of thievery and ignorance, only rarely of murder and fanaticism—a rather important moral fact. Our social system has its fair share of inequity and inhumanity, but it contains no concentration camps and no slavery. If these observations may seem halfhearted to the ardent patriot (and probably treasonable to the nationalist), they should suffice to make clear that our viewpoint is quite incompatible with a radical rejection of American social reality as such. We cannot, therefore, address ourselves meaningfully to those who would see themselves as radicals in this sense. We can speak only to those who, despite all criticisms, would affirm the possibility of moral and political commitment within this American situation.

If one takes this position, a quite viable defense of our religious establishment could be made. It would go something like this: Let us accept the validity of the sociological analysis made in this essay so far. We hardly find it cause for much concern.

The sociologist will be the first to say that any society needs integrating symbols. So does ours. As a result of historical circumstances, the churches have come to take on this function in our society in the way described. Well, so what? If our society, in this world of relativities, is not such a bad thing, why shouldn't it be supported? And what is so terrible about the churches' doing this? And, again, if our society is not inherently evil, why shouldn't the churches help individuals to adjust to it and live in it with a measure of happiness, tolerance, and acceptance? We may well want to make some changes, where we can, especially in those cases where the churches support social inequalities— such as in the case of racial segregation. But all of this is not exactly alarming. Nor is it necessary to take at face value the religious statements made from the pulpit. Nobody expects a minister to admit that he doesn't really know about such things; but, then, few ministers really expect their congregations to take seriously all the traditional elements of the religion they represent. We can be reasonable about this. And even those of us whose personal tastes do not run in the direction of organized religion and who feel no personal need for the sort of symbols that the churches have to offer can look upon all this with a great deal of tolerance. It certainly does not do any harm. The intelligent participant in American society would then do well to turn to more profitable projects than that of revitalizing or reforming the religious institutions. There are many possibilities of moral engagement both at home and abroad. Let us participate in church life, if such is our inclination. Let us be tolerant of those who do, if it is not. And let us leave further studies of the matter to sociologists who have nothing better to do.

Such a defense not only is viable from any more or less positive viewpoint concerning American society but also, in these or similar terms, is commonly made by intelligent people in our situation. Very probably it comes close to the actual thinking of many people who are themselves active members of churches and synagogues. Perhaps not every part of this defense is altogether convincing. For instance, what we have said in our analysis about the ideological and psychological aspects of American religion may put a question mark behind the statement that "it certainly does not do any harm." There may be cases where quite tangible harm is done. But we would not quarrel here over details. Let us grant that such a defense is possible. But let us immediately ask this: What does this defense of our religious establishment leave out? Our answer will be quite simple: It leaves out the Christian faith.

The defense can be made from a purely secularist point of view—even an agnostic or atheistic point of view—provided that it is capable of a degree of tolerance. The defense can also be made from a very vague, very general conception of religion as a barely delineated supernatural background to the real business of living. Our churches can then be accepted as an essentially harmless ingredient of a social reality that we are willing to live with. There is one crucial assumption, however, that we must be willing to abandon—namely, the assumption that these churches have anything to do with the message of the New Testament and the historic creed of Christianity. We can even put this more broadly (in an "interfaith" manner, if you like). We must even abandon the assumption that these churches (or snyagogues) have anything to do with the message of the Old Testament and the historic experience of the Hebrew people. If we are unwilling to abandon these assumptions, our defense collapses. For then we must confront the social magic of our religious institutions with that terrible God who, as early as those distant days when Moses went out to meet Him in the desert, refused to be used for the magical purposes of either individuals or groups. If we wish to hold on to the assumption that our religious institutions have anything to do with this God— the God of Kadesh and of Golgotha—then our religious establishment is brought face to face with the most awesome question there is—namely, the question of blasphemy. And our religious life is placed radically under the condemnation of the first commandment of the Decalogue.

The writer of this essay is unwilling to assume that our churches

have become emancipated from the necessity of this confrontation. He believes that those who have the temerity to call
themselves Christians will have to confront their claims with the
person of Jesus Christ. He even believes that in those places
where the Gospel of Christ is proclaimed in word and sacrament
the presence of this Christ becomes reality—whether those engaged in the proclamation wish it or even believe it. The re-
mainder of this essay is likely to be pretty meaningless to those
not sharing this belief. For those who do, our argument must
now turn from analysis of what is to a delineation of what
ought to be done. It is this that we propose to do now in
discussing what we have called the task of disestablishment.

IV

The Task of Disestablishment

7

The Task of Personal Conversion

The Christian who asks himself what he ought to do in our American situation faces a number of tasks. Some of these are in the realm of consciousness, others in that of action. Before we look at the intellectual and practical problems connected with this, however, there is a very personal aspect of the matter that ought to be looked at first. And, in doing so, we shall once more keep in mind the principal audience to which this essay is addressed—the concerned Christian student.

Christian tradition, ever since the New Testament, has spoken of conversion as the decisive turning point that occurs in a human life as a result of encountering the message of Jesus Christ. This is perhaps a dangerous term to use in America, evoking associations with hysterical revivalism and, even worse, with the streamlined versions of the revivalistic phenomenon in our own time. But little would be accomplished if we tried to think up another term to replace the traditional one. It should be clear that, when we speak of conversion, we are thinking of neither the emotional orgies of the gospel tent, nor the refined editions of these around chilly campfires, nor the fluorescent-lighted mass rallies. Nor would we imply that the encounter with the Christian message must be a sudden, catastrophic experience. There are many roads to Damascus, and some are very slow and

indirect roads. What we do imply in using the term is that the encounter with the Christian faith demands a radical decision. It
confronts us with a message and a demand that claim divine
authority. It raises a vital question of truth. We must decide
whether to believe in the truth of this message and whether to
accept the demands it makes on our existence. We also imply in
using this term that the encounter with the Christian faith is with
something outside of ourselves. The Christian faith is not a mystical path into the mysterious depths of our own being. Indeed, the
Christian faith might seriously question whether we possess any
such depths. The mystery to which it points is an external one.
It lies in history, not in psychology. It tells us that the God who
created the distant nebulae, the God who is other than anything
we can imagine, has come to us; that His coming gives redeem-
ing meaning to our finite existence; and that this meaning may
be found in the life, death, and resurrection of Jesus Christ.
The eyes of the Christian faith look not inward into itself but
outward towards this man Jesus, of whom the New Testament
speaks and who asked this question of His early followers: "Who
do you say that I am?" Conversion to the Christian faith is the
answer to this question, the one once given by Simon Peter—
the stupendous affirmation that the man asking the question is
Christ, the savior. It is the decisive act of God's breaking into
history. We are not concerned here with the many ways in
which the answer may be given—confidently, haltingly, in joy,
or in trepidation—or with the innumerable possibilities of intellectual elaboration of its meaning. Nor can this essay concern
itself with why such an answer might be given. We are not
writing an apologetic for the Christian faith. We are only asking
what the implications of this faith are in our American situation.
And here we confront a massive problem, the dimensions of
which, we would contend, may be found in our previous analysis.

The problem is, quite simply, the effectiveness with which
our religious establishment is designed to prevent the encounter
with the Christian message. We would hasten to add that, from
the viewpoint of the Christian faith, no historical circumstance

can ever prevent the divine invasion of which Christ is the bearer. The risen savior enters through locked doors. But this does not change the fact that doors *may* be locked. A religious establishment in which Christianity is part and parcel of the general value system is a locked door of enormous proportions.

We are saying nothing new. We would refer the reader to Kierkegaard's attack on the "Christendom" of his time or to Barth's assault on a later model of which theological liberalism was the expression. We can, however, explicate this point in terms of our analysis of our own situation. In the American religious-secular continuum of values, Christianity appears embedded in taken-for-granted reality. It does not stand out from the rest of the culture, at least not in its middle-class Protestant forms. Consequently, it can offer no challenge to all that is taken for granted. As we have seen, commitment to Christianity thus undergoes a fatal identification with commitment to society, to respectability, to the American way of life. Under these conditions, the encounter with the Christian message is rendered extremely difficult, to say the least.

The family-centered and child-centered religiosity of many of our suburban middle-class churches contributes greatly to this problem. The ideology of religious education (not to mention such ill-starred side effects as the religious adaptations of psychotherapy and "group dynamics") gives intellectual rationalization to this constellation. What happens, we would argue, is quite obvious. There occurs a process of religious inoculation, by which small doses of Christianoid concepts and terminology are injected into consciousness. By the time the process is completed, the individual is effectively immunized against any real encounter with the Christian message. In most cases, this presumably coincides with the stage in life when people become church members. The act of religious affiliation may thus be, in fact, the final ratification of a religious posture resolutely turned away from the possibility of conversion. Since the entire process is part of socially constituted reality and actually parades under Christian flags, the significance of what has happened may never enter the consciousness of the individual in question. Needless to say, it does not enter the consciousness of those who professionally administer the process. The ideology under whose auspices this travesty occurs is very fond of organic analogies to the religious life. It likes to speak of "nurture," "growth," "maturation." And, in an unintended sense, the ideology is correct. In such a process the individual really "matures." He becomes a well-functioning, well-adjusted adult in the American culture. Religion is a sentimental accompaniment of this socialization. The ideology is equally fond of emphasizing the "group" character of this process. The individual "matures" within the various natural collectivities of his milieu—family, peer group, school—and eventually, heaven help him, within the specific "group experience" which his religious educators provide for him in the church basement. That these natural groupings should be identified with the *koinonia* spoken of in the New Testament is, of course, as absurd sociologically as it is offensive theologically. A group will socialize in terms of the values prevalent in that group. And we have seen what those values are.

It is perhaps an encouraging sign of the persistence of man's religious quest that the contradiction between this social reality and the Christian faith read in the Scriptures (if not preached at all times from the pulpit) has become disturbing to many people in our churches—as it was to the little girl in Park Forest who told her mother, "I don't want to learn about how Christian people live. I want to learn about God."[1] But the whole tenor of our culture, with its systematic avoidance of ecstasy, militates against a break through this religiously guaranteed "O.K. world" into an encounter with the shattering message of the Christian faith. It is culturally appropriate to belong to groups, *not* to adhere to the *koinonia* of the catacombs; to deal with one's guilt, *not* to face one's sin; to grow up into adulthood, *not* to turn on one's way and seek God; to develop a mature mind, *not* to seek the mind of Christ. Now, it is certainly true that no human culture is so designed as to facilitate conversion. The Jewish culture of Jesus' own time was not so designed. Neither was the Graeco-Roman world into which the Christian message was carried by Paul. In other words, the Christian faith will always be in tension with the world. What is characteristic of our situation is that the religious establishment itself obscures this tension and produces the illusion that what tension there is can be understood as growing pains.

Again, we would be careful not to circumscribe the conditions under which God's grace can enter a human life. However, speaking empirically, we would suppose that conversion to the Christian faith in our situation will likely involve a break through the social-psychological functionality of the religious establishment. Furthermore, we would suppose that this break-through is also likely to be associated with at least a measure of alienation from the "O.K. world" of the culture. To say the least, it is difficult to imagine how the religiously mature, socially respectable, and psychologically adjusted church member in our situation can come to terms with the naked horror of Calvary or the blazing glory of Easter morning. Both his religion and his culture compel him to sentimentalize, neutralize, assimilate these Christian images. If he did not do so, they would challenge his religiosity and his respectability and might even threaten his so-called mental health.

It is far from easy for an individual to tear through the web of comforting fictions in which his culture swaddles him. The writer of this essay has discussed elsewhere how the perception of social fiction relates to the Christian faith in general.[2] We would limit ourselves here to the problem this poses in the American culture. And we would emphasize that the peculiar difficulties that are laid in the way of ecstasy by our "O.K. world" are not insurmountable. There are many Americans, young and not so young, who have "left home." And many have learned that they "can't go home again"—not, of course, physically (though the repeated phenomenon of American exiles is instructive), but in the sense of returning to the taken-for-granted social reality of their past. Just as it has been proved possible to break ecstatically through the confines of an American biography, it has also been proved possible to break through the taken-for-granted character of an American religious upbringing. We can put this more simply. It is possible to become free as an American. It is possible to enter on a passionate search for truth in America. And it is also possible that on this search one may confront the Christian message as if one had never heard it before, as if it had never been camouflaged behind the soothing verbiage of one's Sunday school and droned on as a senseless accompaniment to the real events of one's life. That such spiritual adventure has its social and psychological risks is but the measure of its authenticity.

If we say that an encounter with the Christian faith in our situation is likely to be associated with a measure of alienation from the "O.K. world" and its religious establishment, we are not suggesting that young people concerned with such questions should huddle together in rebel bands (though we could imagine worse fates for them). Nor are we advocating some peculiarly esoteric way of finding religious truth or achieving personal authenticity. We are, however, implying a certain pessimism about those who become caught in the organized channels towards so-called religious experience set up institutionally. These channels are likely to be manipulative, even when they provide "critical discussion." There is a great danger that discussions occurring within the groupings of the religious institution are of the nature of Marxist "autocriticism"; that is, the outcome is "fixed" in advance—not, however, let us hasten to add, by the malice of the organizers, but by the inherent social-psychological logic of such situations. Again, this is not to deny the exceptional cases where passionate and altogether free discussion occurs within such institutional groupings (student groups may be a good case in point, though hardly a general one). All the same, we are pessimistic about those whose search for answers expresses itself exclusively in added activity within religiously defined organizations. We suspect that such activity is undertaken, usually unconsciously, with the motive of carefully avoiding the possibility of such answers as would tear asunder one's "O.K. world."

One then asks many questions, but only seemingly so. In actuality one rests on the answer which the group embodies.

Once more we are not saying anything too unusual here. We are simply saying that intensive involvement in religious activities is no guarantee of encountering the Christian message and that sometimes it may be a device protecting against such an encounter. We are saying that the search for truth cannot be routinized in a "program emphasis" by any organization and cannot be realized by the individual by affiliation with any organization. There are no substitutes for passion and no alibis for ecstasy. He who would freely encounter truth must pay the price of being alone. We realize that this price seems exceptionally high for Americans, who are indoctrinated in an ideology of "togetherness" practically from infancy. But then youth is the time when risks are more readily taken. We would once more, as we have done before, emphasize the importance of the student years for the task of achieving authenticity in one's religious positions as well as in other matters. We would reject any short cuts in this task and urge only the courage to intellectual adventure. In these years, if at no other time, there must be the willingness to search for meaning in the far reaches of the world and of the mind—and this means a quest for as much awareness as one is capable of and an honest confronting of as many ideas and modes of existence as one's span of attention can encompass. It means a resolute rejection of what some psychologists have called "closure" and a precipitate commitment to answers that will alleviate one's anxieties—answers that one has not honestly arrived at oneself.

Our pessimism about the organized channels provided for such searching by the religious institution is, of course, grounded in our previous analysis of the religious establishment. We have argued that its social-psychological character offers a standing invitation to inauthenticity. A negative witness to our position on this is afforded by the anti-religious protest. In Europe this protest is frequently vocal and public. Individuals and entire groups (for instance, among intellectuals or in the working classes) will openly reject with contempt what they would regard as the easy road to mental security that leads into the religious institutions. It ought to be stressed very strongly that this is not at all restricted to the circles of Marxists and their sympathizers. Contemporary European literature is full of this vigorous anti-religious protest, which sometimes (as in the writings of Albert Camus) will bracket Communism along with the more traditional religious delusions. In America this protest is usually silent, more polite, expressing itself in withdrawal rather than in assault. But it is real nonetheless.

The protest may be found in the colorful obscenities whispered by soldiers herded into an auditorium to listen to a lecture on "character guidance" given by a military chaplain. It is the core of inner integrity of a skid-row derelict who will bear the shame of taking the supper but not of singing for it. It lies in the anger of a suburban housewife, one of the millions of our unchurched population, finally breaking out against the one visitor too many trying to entice her into his religious fellowship. It lies in the look exchanged between individuals hardly knowing but recognizing each other as they witness some particularly bombastic exhibition of our religio-political oratory. It sometimes finds expressions in the jokes we tell about our clergy. Occasionally it comes to the fore more explicitly in literary expression. This rejection of religion is an important element of what we may call "the other America," that America which is denied and repressed in the "community of the respectable." The geography of obscene language would be a good guide to the sociology of this "other America," as the geography of so-called clean language would define the province of the religious establishment. But such a geography of language would find itself broader in its scope than would a geography of such enclaves of the "other America" as military barracks, poolrooms, and houses of ill repute. The geography of language would have to concern itself with the eruptions of linguistic protest in the late hours of business conventions or in the release of jazz sessions. Wherever this language is found, the clergyman is out of place and is instinctively and sometimes violently felt as the symbol of inauthenticity. In terms of our analysis, this phenomenon is not difficult to understand.

Needless to say, we are not interested in promoting the use of profanity. We are only suggesting that religion is symptomatically out of place on those occasions when Americans try to shake off the weight and the pretenses of social propriety. In language, as in roles, religion belongs to the domain of the "clean and proper." It is thus morally fitting that the language of the pulpit is most kin to the language of the political platform.

It would be very difficult to prove such a proposition, but we would go out on a limb and speculate that the proportion of unchurched individuals is very high among those who have achieved a degree of emancipation from the major social fictions. The writer of this essay is being admittedly impressionistic here. But he would invite the reader to compare his own impressions with this proposition. If one imagines an individual who has been disenchanted with the "official" interpretations of reality, who is skeptical of the mass-communicated ideals of the market place, who with much effort and perhaps a good deal of anguish has arrived at his own view of society—if one compares this image with people one has known who come more or less close to it—how easily can one then imagine such an individual in a Protestant church on Sunday morning? We would contend that at this point our imagination will become strained. The religious milieu of our establishment is not congenial to this type. The social skeptic (let alone the social rebel) will have to seek his community elsewhere. And the Protestant church of our imagination would have to be a rather unusual one or would have to change very much from the norm if it were to welcome such individuals.

To repeat: we dare not delimit the movements of grace. The Christian message, in the power of the Holy Spirit, can blaze its path into a human heart even through regiments of smiling ushers with flowered lapels and underneath a pulpit from which comes nothing, Sunday after Sunday, but the platitudes gleaned from canned sermon outlines. However, we are venturing to suggest that Christian conversion also has a social dimension. Surely Jesus did not mean to exclude the rich from the Kingdom of God. But He said that being rich made the entrance into that Kingdom much more difficult. And it might have been possible for the Hebrews to encounter their God amid the fleshpots of Egypt. The indicated avenue, however, led them into the desert. Thus, conversion in our own situation is not unusual in having a social dimension. And to repeat once more: We are arguing that a goodly portion of alienation from the "O.K. world" of religious and social settlement will facilitate the encounter with the Christian message. We would also argue that such alienation will likely be a consequence of this encounter. Consequently, personal conversion in our situation cannot be easily identified with ecclesiastical engagement. If this argument is disagreeable to the religious organizers, we regret the inconvenience—and regretfully must stick to our guns.

In a culture where religion is functional both socially and psychologically, Christian preaching itself ought to call men to a confrontation with the God who stands against the needs of society and against the aspirations of the human heart. We shall elaborate this point in the following chapter. Here we would only stress once more that the Christian faith demands a personal decision. No amount of religious "growth" or social involvement in religious groups can release us from this demand. This decision is for Jesus Christ, not for the religious institution. Indeed, the decision for the religious institution can be a flight from the decision that is demanded. But perhaps a prior decision is called for—that is the decision to follow the truth wherever it may lead, to attempt at all times to be an authentic human being, to refuse easy consolations, and to risk the loneliness of saying "no!" to that which is socially established. For the Christian, however, there is a real consolation in this prior decision. If God is truth, He will not leave alone the one who passionately desires truth. In the end, Christian truth and human integrity cannot be contradictory.

8

The Task of Theological Construction

The milieu of our establishment is not favorable to theology, and this means that theologians rarely attain leading positions in the ecclesiastical organizations. This is true in other countries, too. What is more specifically American is the common feeling that theology is an academic discipline with its place in academic settings but with little relevance to the ongoing business of the religious life, institutional as well as personal. Very probably this feeling is to be explained in terms of a much broader anti-intellectualism in America, a subject that has been discussed in many studies of our culture. In the case of American religion, however, the depreciation of intellectual effort has particularly devastating consequences. For theology is the intellectual articulation of the Christian faith. As such, it provides criteria by which both the institutional and the personal aspects of the Christian life can be evaluated. In the absence of theological criteria, two very dangerous criteria will tend to take over—in the institutional area, the criterion of expediency; and in the personal area, that of experience.

Theology provides the self-understanding of the Christian community. Indeed, this is how theology originated in church history. Most often this self-understanding became necessary as the Christian community was confronted with critical challenges from without or with misinterpretations of its message from within. When churches abandon or de-emphasize theology, they give up the intellectual tools by which the Christian message can be articulated and defended. In the resulting chaos of religious ideas, the principal criterion left to the community as it seeks to find its way is, quite naturally, that of expediency. This is very rarely the consequence of deliberate scheming. It is the natural, almost automatic outcome of abandoning the quest for rational clarity.

The writer of this essay is a Lutheran and is quite strongly prejudiced in favor of churches having a confessional or creedal foundation. For this reason it is important to stress that what is being said here is *not* to be construed as a call for the adoption of creedal platforms by our churches. Any creed is a useless ceremony unless it is the product of a passionate intellectual search and a decision of faith by a community of Christians. It is, indeed, a common Lutheran fallacy that subscription to the historic confessions by clergy and congregations provides foolproof protection against intellectual confusion about the faith. There is no alibi for intellectual effort, not even the Augsburg Confession. The historic confessions can be priceless instruments in the service of theological self-understanding. They can also be hollow rhetoric giving an illusion of profundity and, simultaneously, a license for not thinking any further. If the latter is the case, they assist rather than hinder the dominion of expediency.

To repeat our contention: Theology provides criteria by which Christian churches can judge themselves. If these criteria are lost, the Christian faith becomes the night in which all cats are gray. Manipulation of the tradition for institutional ends takes the place of the effort to articulate, reinterpret, and reapply the tradition. The primary criterion of institutional action will then tend to be expediency.

The corruption of expediency, as a direct consequence of intellectual inertia, has its very personal side as well. We can find illustrations of this, with frightening frequency, not only among laymen but also among the clergy. Among seminary students the beginning of this corruption is marked by a subtle but far-reaching change of interest in the subject matter of the curriculum. One is no longer interested in the question, "What is the truth?" One asks instead, "How can I preach this?" Theological questions will have relevance only as rationalizations of professionally required acts or, even worse, as a bag of rhetorical tricks to play the professional role with effect. When this happens over a period of years, the individual becomes fixated in a permanent posture of dishonesty. Protestants, who frequently and with much justification criticize Catholics for their *sacrificium intellectus* in various matters of faith, would do well to ponder this surrender of intellectual integrity flourishing in their own midst. They might even come to the conclusion that something may be said for sacrificing one's intellect for a dogma believed to be divinely sanctioned as against doing so for the expediency of the institution in which one is embarking on a career.

Be this as it may, the more general personal consequence of the abandonment of theological criteria for the Christian life is the cult of experience. Again, there is little doubt that this emphasis on experience must be seen against the wider background of American culture. Pragmatism in religion is but an example of a more general pattern. In terms of American church history, it is also very likely that we must look for the roots of this cult of experience in the erosion of the Reformation tradition first by the pietism of the various revivals and then (quite possibly in direct consequence) by the development of theological liberalism. We are not concerned here, however, with historical explanations. We would only submit what is essentially a very simple proposition: When an individual ceases to grapple intellectually with the problems posed by his religion, feeling takes the place of thought. Another substitution of questions takes place here. The individual no longer asks, "What is the truth?" Instead, he asks "What do I feel?" And that is but one step to the next question: "How does this make me feel?" Emotional pragmatism now takes the place of the honest confrontation with the Christian message. The way is opened for the attitude of the religious consumer, who shops around the denominational supermarket for just the right combination of spiritual kicks and thrills to meet his particular psychological needs. The question of truth loses all significance.

The task of theological construction is especially important in the American situation because of the widespread domination by the criteria of expediency and experience. Theological construction means neither a return to empty traditional formulas nor the concoction of glittering pronunciamentos with which the religious institutions can make a splash in the publicity media. It means rather a return to painstaking and passionate intellectual effort, the willingness to confront the Christian faith with all the critical faculties of the mind and to find the means to articulate this faith in our own historical moment. Needless to say, this task, like any systematic intellectual enterprise, requires the *expertise* of some. Yet theology cannot be left to the experts. The layman will need the guidance and the scholarly equipment of the theologian. But, as a thinking human being, he will have to make his own intellectual decisions.

The writer of this essay must disclaim competence as a theological scholar. He is a sociologist, not a theologian, and must approach these questions as a layman. Therefore, it cannot be our intention here to develop a program for the task of theological construction that is required. But what we can do is to look back at our analysis of the American religious situation and at least see in what way this analysis may be relevant to the theological task at hand. We can do this by looking once more at the fourfold establishment analyzed before, beginning with the last aspect discussed.

Some indications of the theological task involved in the psychological establishment have already been given in the preceding chapter. We would contend once more that it is imperative in this context to elaborate theologically the nonmystical and, even more, the nonpsychological character of the Christian faith, since psychological experience has become a sort of common man's mysticism. The exegesis of the Old Testament is perhaps even more important in this connection than that of the New. This means the explication of the externality of the Biblical encounter with God. The God we meet in the Bible is the God of history, not of so-called religious experience. It is He who comes to seek out man, not man who can lift his soul up to the divine heights. Indeed, what man finds on the heights is only the idols of his own imagination. Nor can this God be used for human purposes, magical or political or emotional. The God of Moses, who refused to give His name for magical use, is the same God who comes to us in Jesus Christ. When we want to use God today for our psychological needs, we repeat in modern form the same blasphemy which in ancient times wanted to appropriate Him magically. God will not let Himself be used—not for the political purposes of Israel and not for the emotional purposes of latter-day Israelites.

A theological understanding of the Biblical message will make it impossible to let the Christian faith become psychological religion in the manner analyzed. God is not a psychological palliative. When the attempt is made to use Him as one, the Christian theologian ought to welcome wholeheartedly the debunking tools put at his disposal by the Marxist and Freudian critics of religion. The Christian faith, however, cannot be either a social or an individual opiate. On the contrary, when it remains true to itself it will shatter the "O.K. worlds" in which people seek shelter from the terrors of existence. It will not prevent ecstasy; rather, it will force the individual into the most radical ecstasy possible, that of confrontation with the living God. Such terms as "social adjustment" or "mental health" will then be seen to be without significance in the Christian frame of reference.

We are certainly not implying here that the Christian faith has some peculiar affinity to lunacy or that in order to become a Christian one ought to become what modern psychiatrists call a neurotic. We are only saying that these psychological factors are irrelevant to the Christian faith. Also, when we emphasize that God is the one who stands over against our needs, we are not denying the classical Christian affirmation that man exists ultimately for and towards God, that (in Augustine's words) he is restless until he rests in God. Of course, any Christian would maintain that, in a profound sense, all men need God. But we must not confound this ultimate need with the needs diagnosed by our psychologists. God is the final answer to the question of man's existence. He is not the answer to man's needs for emotional balance, marital happiness, or getting along with his fellows. Even a cursory glance at the figures we meet in the Bible and in church history ought to convince us of this. We may speculate on how Ezekiel would come out on balance and Paul on happiness. And it may even be relevant to remind our religious mental hygienists that Jesus of Nazareth was crucified— no doubt the logical outcome of a maladjusted and self-punishing biography.

The reminder of the earthly life of Jesus and its theological implications may also serve to deal with the social establishment of religion. We need to remind ourselves that the early followers of Jesus were among the despised and perhaps even the despicable in the land. For there may be some inverse social snobbery possible in admiring simple rustics, but there is nothing easily admirable in prostitutes and collaborators with a national enemy. In any case, there is little doubt that the early Christians would have been out of place in what was then nice, proper, respectable society. Nor can we take lightly what Jesus said about these segments of the population. It is hardly just a matter of proletarian romanticism if we suspect that Jesus Christ continues to walk the dark alleys of our society rather than its bright boulevards. Nor is it romanticism if we suspect that the propriety that characterizes our middle-class churches shuts out Christ along with those who, like his early disciples, bear the marks of shame and oppression.

We hear very much today about the sin of racial segregation in the churches. We agree very strongly. But we would add that class segregation is sin, too—also if it should now choose to de-emphasize racial divisions. As a result of the ecumenical movement, we also hear very much these days about the sin and the scandal of Christian disunity. And we would agree on this also. But the fact that Presbyterians and Methodists are separated from each other is no more a scandal than the separation of the classes in each of these two denominations. To a sociologist, there is some irony in the fact that within the ecumenical movement there is now much discussion of the "non-theological factors" in the disunity of the churches, welcome though such discussion is. The sociologist is likely to feel that the separations caused by these factors are far more serious than those caused by theological disagreement. After all, from a purely human point of view, it is less scandalous to separate because one honestly disagrees about religious truth than because the United States census puts one in different income brackets. What is more, the sociologist (as we have seen) will feel that such economic facts weigh more heavily in the real life of institutions than the theological quarrels of which most church members are blissfully unaware.

The social establishment of religion in America thus puts to us a direct question of sin, just as much as does the matter of racial segregation, although it is probably true that the latter is more appalling in terms of the hurt and humiliation inflicted on its individual victims. Thus, when we speak about sin, we might accuse a theology professor at Princeton for despising a colleague at Drew. For the rank-and-file Presbyterian, however, the sin is much more likely to be one of social contempt than of intellectual pride. And when we remember that Jesus prayed that Christians should be one, we suspect that this prayer has applicability not only to, say, Canterbury and Rome, but also to the slums and suburbia. And if we are concerned with the scandal to unbelievers, we suspect that the latter case is more important.

There is both a theological and a sociological problem in the fact that the Christian community exists empirically in a society which already contains a great variety of other communities to which the Christian also belongs.[1] We cannot go into this problem here. Suffice it to say that it would be very naïve (again, both theologically and sociologically) to think that all human social identifications will disappear miraculously when men come together in the name of Christ. The one, holy, catholic Church is an object of faith, not an empirical datum. And we must acknowledge our own sin which keeps it divided and unholy. But our immediate question is not how far we may hope for sociological miracles. It is rather how far we dare regard as a norm the state of affairs which our sin brings about. It is here that the task of theological construction must begin in this matter.

Very likely it is in a doctrine of the Church that theology would be most relevant to the problem of the social establishment. By defining what the Church ought to be and already is as the body of Christ, theology can provide the criteria by which the empirical reality can be evaluated. Another warning might be in place here. In this matter it is very important that theological articulation be accompanied by empirical perception. If the latter is absent (a common state of affairs), it is very possible that the theological doctrine is misunderstood as a factual description— and thus, from being a criterion of judgment, the doctrine becomes an instrument of rationalization. It is not enough, in other words, to have a doctrine of the Church. One must also have a sociology of the empirically existent churches. A Christian view of our situation can then emerge from the tension between theological doctrine and sociological diagnosis. The diagnosis without the doctrine may lead to resignation, which is bad, but the doctrine without the diagnosis almost certainly leads to illusion, which is much worse.

Of the four aspects analyzed in our religious establishment, the political aspect probably falls most sharply under the judgment of the Biblical witness. And here we can safely begin with Amos. The God of the prophetic message stands sovereignly above all nations and empires. He cannot be invoked as a safe political ally —not even by Israel. The confidence that He will not abandon Israel to defeat and disaster is an illusion. Indeed, it may even be that the Assyrians or Babylonians are the instruments of His purpose in history. Living in a country that faces a particularly frightening kind of Assyrians today and very fond of comforting itself with a variety of "days of prayer," we would do well to begin our thoughts in this area with what Amos has to say about the nature of the "day of the Lord."[2] The people who would make of God an ideological weapon in our political conflicts are engaged in blasphemy. This cannot be said strongly enough. And the Biblical witness also allows us to say that one blasphemes against God at one's own peril.

What we have said in our analysis of political religion about the parallels between our American situation and that which the early Christians faced in the Roman Empire is surely a matter of theological significance. Perhaps we might arrive at the considered judgment that these Christian martyrs were wrong in feeling so strongly about their Imperial cult. In any case, we must come to theological grips with the existence of our own facsimile of it. We suspect that, if this theological task became a widespread concern in our churches, there would come about a marked retreat of our clergy from the ceremonies of the religio-political cult. And, very logically, there might come about some decrease in the public prestige and prominence of organized religion. We also suspect that such secularization of our political life would have to be welcomed from the viewpoint of the Biblical witness.

The above considerations would apply in very similar fashion to a theological critique of our cultural religion. Just as the Christian faith cannot be readily identified with a particular political creed, it cannot be identified with a particular culture's value system. As soon as this happens, the prophetic mission of the Church is paralyzed from the start. We suspect that any situation in which the Church exits in a culture without any noteworthy tension provides a danger signal that something seems to be radically wrong. That is, we suspect that the very nature of the Christian faith precludes the complete absence of tension within a culture. This, of course, does not mean that Christians will always be persecuted in a violent way. There are many ways of being eaten by lions. But a situation in which the Christians are indistinguishable from all the other spectators in the cultural coliseum is hardly one in which we would find much faithfulness to the example of the crucified savior.

These are very general considerations. If we would now subject the American values previously analyzed to a theological critique, we dare say that their identification with the Christian faith will appear as an impossibility. This-wordliness, moralism, success, activism, conformity to cultural norms, suppression of metaphysical concerns—all these are values that must be in tension with the Christian view of the human condition. Again, looking at the earthly life of Jesus should suffice to make this clear, even before any further theological elaboration. Jesus of Nazareth was one who proclaimed that the Kingdom of God was not of this world. He broke the sabbath. He associated with those outside the norms of the culture of that day. And in human terms his life was a total failure. We suspect that it is a theological task in our situation to elaborate the eschatological character of the Christian faith against the this-wordliness of American religiosity, to set justification by faith against our pervasive legalism, to explain the meaning of the cross in a culture that glorifies success and happiness. And we would argue once more that such an understanding of the Christian faith will of necessity lead at least to a measure of alienation from the culture.

In all aspects of our religious establishment, therefore, theological thinking is likely to substitute tension for expediency, as it will replace the hedonism of experience by intellectual passion. Nor should this surprise any honest reader of the New Testament, which, after all, is supposed to be the yardstick of Christian theology. We would certainly not argue that the cross is to be the central focus of Christian thought. Indeed, we believe that the resurrection is the much more important focus. But as far as the theological critique of our establishment is concerned, we would strongly advocate a *theologia crucis*. Perhaps the first proposition of such a theological critique might be that there is no mystical symbolism about the cross. It just happened to be the Roman instrument of execution. Perhaps a liturgical reform in our situation that is not just an activity of aesthetic titillation, but is worship grounded in the Gospel, might make a timely substitution here. It would be an interesting experience, to say the least, to have one of our suburban congregations troop into its sanctuary one Sunday morning and find on the altar, between the flowers and the flag, a gilded miniature of the electric chair. For those with "high-church" inclinations, we would suggest that the figure in the electric chair be that of a Negro. The pastor responsible for this little liturgical innovation might have some difficulty completing his building-fund campaign, but on that morning he would have an excellent opportunity to preach the Gospel.

Various observers have pointed out that the relationship between religion and culture in America today is very similar to that which existed in Europe before the rise of the totalitarian movements. The development of the Protestant churches in Germany, through their experience with Nazism and Communism, is probably the best example of a transformation from a taken-for-granted identification with culture to a consciousness of tension. Especially the documents that emerged in the churches' struggle with Nazism in the early 1930s deserve close attention by American Christians today. We might take as an example the following statements from the Barmen Declaration of 1934, which became the theological rallying point of the Confessing Church movement:

We repudiate the false teaching that there are areas of our life in which we belong not to Jesus Christ but another lord, areas in which we do not need justification and sanctification through him. . . .
We repudiate the false teaching that the church can turn over the form of her message and ordinances at will or according to some dominant ideological and political convictions. . . .
We repudiate the false teaching that the church, in human self-esteem, can put the word and work of the Lord in the service of some wishes, purposes and plans or other, chosen according to desire.[3]

While other statements of the time obviously are relevant only to the situation then encountered by German Christians, the above "repudiations," quite as they stand, are applicable to our own situation. We are fortunate to live in a society in which there is no totalitarian tyranny and in which the Christian faith can be proclaimed freely. But the very benign climate of our situation also tends to blur the distinctions—which is why we can learn from those who witnessed under oppression.

The existence of the Church under Communist totalitarianism has created new problems, some similar to and some different from those encountered under Nazism. Yet the insight of the sovereignty of God over all cultural forms emerges just as clearly from that situation. Even if we must have serious reservations about some of Karl Barth's political judgments on the question of Communism, the following passage from a letter of his to Christians in the Communist part of Germany also has its relevance for ourselves in our own situation:

The church's existence does not always have to possess the same form in the future that it has possessed in the past, as though this were the only possible pattern. . . . The continuance and victory of the cause of God, which the Christian Church is to serve with her witness, is not unconditionally linked with the forms of existence which it has had until now. Yes, the hour may strike and has perhaps already struck when God, to our discomfiture, but to his glory and for the salvation of mankind, will put an end to this mode of existence because it lacks integrity and has lost its usefulness. Yes, it could be our duty to free ourselves inwardly from our dependency on that mode of existence even while it lasts. Indeed, on the assumption that it may one day entirely disappear, we definitely should look about us for new ventures in new directions.[4]

We are not suggesting that American Christians should ape the course of Christians in other countries. However, one of the fruits of ecumenical contacts has been the possibility of learning from one another. And on this particular point we have much to learn from the European churches and possibly also from those in what used to be called the missionary countries. The learning will not be simple imitation if we push forward to the basic theological problems implicit in their actions as well as ours.

We have deliberately refrained in this chapter from making references to specific theological works. This essay is not a theological treatise. However, we would make clear that when we speak of a theological task ahead of us we do not wish to imply that this task must now begin from a *tabula rasa*. The task has already begun in a very real sense, and for this we owe a particular debt of gratitude to what is popularly called the "neo-orthodox movement." The term is ambiguous and can include a most heterogeneous crowd indeed. But even its popular usage has merit if the common element in this intellectual movement is seen to be the renewed attempt to understand the Christian message theologically, an understanding that finds itself in tension with the prevailing cultural religiosity. This common element can be found in the continuing appeal of Barthian theology, in the work of the two Niebuhrs and of Paul Tillich, in the growing interest in this country in the work of Dietrich Bonhoeffer, and even in the efforts of those who would rediscover the theological genius of a particular confessional tradition, such as the Anglican or the Lutheran. Those who see the necessity of a radical theological critique of American religious life may have an agony of choice between these various possibilities, but at least they have the comfort of not having to begin their task *ex nihilo*. Perhaps one of the most urgent parts of this task is to make clear to a wider Protestant public that theology is not intended to be an esoteric pastime of incomprehensible intellectuals. Theology belongs to the Christian Church and thus ought to be the concern of the Christian laity—the people, the *laos,* of that Church. And certainly those (such as Christian students) who pride themselves on their intellectual intrepidity in other areas cannot afford to relegate the theological task in its entirety to the experts, however welcome the special gifts of the latter might be.

The variety of theological paths mentioned in the preceding paragraph should help to avoid the impression that we are concluding here with a special plea for some theological position or for "neo-orthodoxy" in general. The writer of this essay must admit to having had his own difficulties with some who call themselves "neo-orthodox"—sometimes with their intellectual arrogance, sometimes with their unwillingness to look at empirical reality or with their all too ready equation of the Church affirmed in the creeds with the social institution of that name. To say that we owe a debt of gratitude to "neo-orthodoxy" is not a call for hoisting a party flag. Indeed, no "movement" can offer us affiliation with intellectual integrity. Persons who think alike will naturally find each other in groups, and this is as it should be. But the task of theological construction begins in the consciousness of each individual Christian. Our only special plea is for the courage to think, ruthlessly if need be. Theological thinking is always a venture of both faith and intellect, more so than thinking in many other areas because of the tremendous importance of its subject matter. This is why this venture is particularly needed in our American situation.

9

The Task of Social Engagement

As we have seen before, the proposition that the churches are socially irrelevant is not necessarily disturbing from an enlightened secularist point of view. A person holding such a point of view can well afford to be tolerant of the religious activities of his fellow citizens and can even admit that these activities may do some good occasionally while his own social concerns find expression in purely secular channels. This tolerance of the churches' social irrelevance will be even more benevolent if one takes a basically positive attitude towards American society. One might then even feel a certain irritation with people who radically criticize a major institution of the society and might suggest to them that they could vent their reformist urges on more significant matters—such as the struggle for racial justice, or the problems of ethical responsibility in the business community, or the fight for democracy in the underdeveloped areas of the world and America's stake in that fight. We are repeating ourselves on this point. But the repetition is worth while to stress once more that we are not asking for social relevance on the part of the churches because we feel that American society is terrible or because of some general prejudice against conservative institutions. Even museums have their place. And, from the viewpoint of a patriotic and democratic concern for the well-being of American society, there is no particular reason to be alarmed if the American churches, sociologically speaking, turn out to be museums. Swedish democracy has not suffered by the prevalence of secularism and Portuguese democracy has not derived much benefit from the prevailing religiosity. We ask rather for social relevance on the part of the churches because we have a Christian bias concerning what the churches ought to be. The social relevance of the Christian community is not a political imperative. The current propaganda in this regard is to be dismissed as a mystification. The social relevance of the Christian community is an imperative only of the Christian faith. It is the nature of the Christian faith, not the nature of society, which calls for the prophetic mission of the Christian community. Christians are called to be the salt of the earth. If they cease to be that, they risk betraying the very purpose of the Church of Jesus Christ. Hendrik Kraemer has said that the Church *is* mission. Perhaps this formulation is too one-sided. But we would certainly agree that the very being of the Church is endangered when the sense of mission dissolves in the vacuum of social irrelevance.

It goes without saying that the Christian faith, even in its Biblical sources, will always appear in historical garb. Just as Christ was incarnate in human flesh, so the Church is always embedded in the relativities of specific cultural situations. To speak of a Christian community free from all cultural and social determination is to indulge in utopianism—and possibly also to misunderstand the nature of the incarnation. But saying this is something quite different from giving assent to the religious establishment existing today in American society. The freedom of the Church does not mean a mystical existence high above the shifting sands of history. No human community can be free in this sense, as sociologists know perhaps better than many others. But freedom means at least a relative choice of courses through the terrain of culture. What is required in our situation is a new sense of the freedom of the Church. A free Church does not mean a community that is radically detached from culture, a sort of un-American enclave living on the margins of society. But a free Church *will* mean a measure of disestablishment. In relating to the culture, a free Church will pick and choose. Neither its affirmation nor its denial of cultural values will be absolute. In such an attitude of freedom the Christian community can then engage itself with the social dynamics of the rapidly changing American situation. Such social engagement may not lead to dramatic changes in the nature of society. But it will mean a change from the passive to the active mood in the churches' relationships with the society. In the measure that this happens, the functionality of the religious institution previously analyzed will be damaged. As, indeed, it should be from the viewpoint of the Christian faith.

If our previous analysis of the place of the religious institution in American society is tenable, then it is especially important to state very modestly one's expectations concerning the possibility and consequences of Christian social engagement. If the functionality of religion in American society is directly related to its social irrelevance, then any attempt to make religion more relevant socially implies going against very powerful forces in the situation. Human beings naturally respond to social expectations. It is exceedingly difficult to deny such expectations. In other words, the major forces of our situation militate against the task of social engagement. Let us hasten to add that this will only rarely mean that the churches face persecution as soon as they try for social relevance. Martyrdom is much more likely to come with a shrug of indifference than with a cry of hatred. We must dismiss heroic fantasies of either variety—both of that which imagines the glory of victory and of that which eagerly expects to be crucified. Our contemporary society is unlikely to give us either satisfaction. In most cases, the task of social engagement will be a slow, difficult, and sometimes tedious job of letting the Christian conscience be heard amid the immense complexities of our social involvements. Such a job requires a rather levelheaded kind of enthusiasm. And at each step of the process one will be up against the most powerful social force there is—the expectations of others around one.

To realize this, however, does not mean that it makes no sense to try. There may even be situations in which it may be a

Christian duty to bang one's head meticulously and systematically against a brick wall. Our situation is probably not quite as Sisyphean as all that. But we have every reason to curb our own expectations as well. The task of social engagement will not be accomplished by presenting the churches with a new gimmick, a new organizational blucprint, or a new "program emphasis." It is even possible that, when we try to fulfil this task, we may find that our present organizations and programs are seriously put in question.

From the foregoing it will be evident that no generally valid formula for a Christian engagement with society can be given. Forms of engagement will vary in different situations in which Christians seek to be relevant to the social reality around them. However, for purposes of discussion, we would differentiate between four major possibilities of such social engagement— Christian diaconate, Christian action, Christian presence, and Christian dialogue. We shall now take up these possibilities in turn. It is not suggested that these constitute some kind of exclusive list. As to giving the most space to the last of these possibilities, the writer of this essay happily admits to a strong bias on this count, though he believes that a viable rationale can be offered for this bias.

Christian diaconate, as one form of relevant engagement with society, has behind it a venerable tradition in church history. It can be defined quite simply as the helping outreach of the Christian community to individuals in distress—those suffering from illness, poverty, or other personal difficulties. Already the New Testament knows of the Christian concern for orphans and widows. Throughout Christian history this concern has extended to the most varied groups suffering in one form or another in their specific social situations—slaves, prisoners, the mentally ill, the old, those subjected to discrimination on account of race or nationality. Such Christian concern, often beginning with an interest in individuals only, has on occasion contributed itself to much broader institutional change—as in this country when Christians were involved in the struggle for the abolition of slavery or in the drive to reform prisons or mental hospitals. This essay is hardly the place to trace the historical development of such Christian diaconate or even to discuss in detail the manifold ways in which American churches engage in social-welfare activities today.[1] The most important point to make in terms of our argument is that, despite contrary criticisms of "social actionists," such Christian diaconate is a fully legitimate form of social engagement and, in all likelihood, will remain so in any conceivable future. This does not mean, of course, that diaconal service in our modern society does not face peculiar problems, especially in countries approximating the type of the "welfare state." Obviously Christians face different diaconal tasks in a country that has no hospitals than in one with an efficient public-health system. In any situation Christians will have to ask themselves what the human needs are and in what way they, as Christians, can make a distinctive contribution. Occasionally an analysis of the situation in these terms may show that distinctively Christian institutions have become obsolete. Again, it is not our job here to discuss such cases in detail.

Since the argument of this essay bases itself on a sociological analysis, it is especially important to stress the legitimacy, from a Christian viewpoint, of the unspectacular and unpretentious concern for individuals that diaconal service involves. Sociologists and other people interested in the broad sweep of social forces are often impatient with those whose concern is limited to the little old lady next door rather than extended to the demographic, social, and political problems of the aged in our society. Against this claim to the larger perspective, however valid it may be on other grounds, Christians must always emphasize the primary importance of the unique individual in his unique need. Modern movements of revolutionary change should serve as a warning against the disregard of individual suffering in the concern for sweeping social transformations.

Without going into these questions in detail, it might be pointed out that the institutionalization and professionalization of what used to be called charity may possibly provide the main opportunity for Christians and Christian churches to make a distinctive diaconal contribution, albeit in a negative way. This is certainly not to be construed as a reactionary criticism of the "welfare state." Mass organization of welfare activities is a necessity of modern mass society, no matter how it is arranged politically. The processes of such organization are visible not only, for example, in public health clinics but also in the over-crowded waiting rooms of physicians in private practice. Nor can professionalization be avoided in a complex society with an increasing need for specialists in every imaginable area of life. We would contend that Christians can make their most distinctive contributions in the interstitial areas of modern wel-fare organization. This is probably most true of Christians in their local congregations. As soon as Christian diaconate be-comes organized in denominational and interdenominational boards of one kind or another, organization of an essentially secular character is likely to take over. Let it be said that this is not meant as a criticism of such boards. Their service will certainly continue to have its justification. But it is unlikely that welfare institutions administered by an ecclesiastical board will differ greatly from those under the control of committees, com-missions, or other agencies without a Christian label. What is distinctively Christian in the concern for suffering men and women is more likely to come out in less organized ways.

A good illustration of this would be the problem of the aged.[2] It goes without saying that this problem cannot be understood as a purely individual one. It must be approached in terms of broad economic and political measures. Indeed, when the prob-lem is approached in purely individual terms, this approach is often nothing but an ideology in the service of vested interests. The American public has had a good taste of such ideology in the propaganda of organized medicine against a national health plan for the aged. When it comes to dealing with these broad implications of the problem, Christian responsibility is better expressed through political participation than in projects ema-nating from the churches themselves. But it is fortunately not too difficult to imagine a situation in which the necessary economic and political measures have been taken. Still, there will remain basic human needs—those coming from the psychological difficulties of retirement in an action-oriented culture, those coming from the social fact that there is no real place for the aged in our modern nuclear family—and, last but not least, the perennial human problems of boredom, loneliness, and the fear of death. These needs and problems are hard to reach through institutional means. Nor (with all due respect to the new field of gerontology) are professionals necessarily the best people to deal with them. It is here that Christians, individually and in congregations, can carry out a very distinctive diaconal service indeed. Christian groups can reject more freely than others the bias of our culture in favor of youth. They can provide places of meaningful activity to the aged, in terms of real service rather than artificially concocted activities. They can provide social situations in which the aged can overcome the segregation all too often inflicted by our society and perhaps even help families to overcome the egotism that uses economic alibis for unthinking cruelty. It is quite possible that volunteers in local congregations (such as young people or housewives) could, by a few hours of service every week, assist old people in remaining independent—in lieu of the meaningless projects that such volunteers often engage in now. None of these things requires new institutions or further professionalization in the services of the local congregation. Yet in these ways a distinctively Christian diaconate can find expression in a spirit that the large welfare organizations of modern society, however efficient and necessary, would have a hard time duplicating.

Christian diaconate will continue to be a relevant response of the Christian community to society as long as there are individuals in physical or mental need of any kind. As society changes, Christian diaconate requires imagination and courage in seeking out new ways of service. It can probably be said that American Protestantism has no reason to be particularly embarrassed about its efforts in this direction. Nor is there any reason for self-castigation on the part of those concerned with diaconal service in its varied forms. There can be no doubt about the Christian legitimacy of this kind of social engagement. However, it must be asked whether this kind can be the only kind.

If one gains a little distance from the immediate cases that concern one, individual suffering of the kind that calls for diaconal service may look like the debris of social structure. But it is obvious that clearing away the debris does not change the structure. Indeed, in some instances this very alleviation of individual distress may strengthen the institution that is the root cause of the distress. For example, a social worker employed in a situation in which labor is exploited may indirectly assist in the perpetuation of this state of affairs. He helps one individual here and a family there, thereby helping to control resentments against the over-all situation and to avoid radical changes in that situation. Thus, the employment of social workers, industrial chaplains, and other "human relations" experts has served in quite a few industrial situations as a tool of management to prevent the growth of aggressive unionism. It may be pointed out in passing that this possible conservative function of social work in all its forms must also be taken into consideration when one tries to evaluate Christian diaconate in any specific situation. For example, in the American South the question may well be raised whether the efforts put into diaconal-type work among Negroes have not willy-nilly contributed to the maintenance of the segregation system and whether Christians ought not rather engage their energies in the political struggle for racial equality. Christians in similar situations may well decide that both courses of action are called for—the broadside attack on the entire social structure and the work of alleviation among individuals suffering under that structure. The important consequence of this consideration for our argument is that sometimes the latter course without the former course may be ethically ambiguous.

Christian action may be defined as any attempt not only to deal with individuals but also to try to modify the social structure itself. Another way of putting this is to say that such action will try to induce social change in some direction thought desirable from the viewpoint of Christian ethics. In the American situation this will usually mean the kind of activity that has come to be known as "social action," that is, the mobilization of Christians as groups or individuals within the political processes of democracy. The typical course of events here will consist of the formation of committees that will seek to organize political propaganda and will put pressure on governmental agencies to pass a certain bill, or to revoke a certain practice, or to initiate or terminate a certain program. What is done here from a Christian motivation will not be different politically from similar actions carried on by groups without this motivation. The typical form of such action is political struggle within the framework of our democratic institutions—political parties, legislatures, various branches of government, the media of public communication, and so on.

However, while this is the normal form of Christian action as we have defined it in our American situation, it is important to point out that such democratic participation is not necessarily the only possible form. Even in America this is so. For example, the strategy of the recent "sit-ins" in the South is action in the sense of our definition, yet it means deliberately stepping outside the framework of democratic politics into open resistance to a situation deemed fundamentally unjust. The same can be said about the practices of nonviolent resistance of pacifist groups in this country. In these cases action means not only trying to change the laws (which is in accordance with democratic theory) but also, if necessary, to defy them (which is not so in accordance). In this country, even those who find themselves constrained by their Christian conscience to engage in illegal acts have limited themselves to nonviolent forms of resistance.

There have been situations where Christian action, still within our definition, has led to violence. For example, the decision of some Christians to participate in the revolutionary conspiracy against the Nazi regime in 1944 was motivated by the conviction that in that particular situation nothing short of violence would meet the demands of Christian responsibility for one's neighbors. The same was true of the decision of Christians to participate in the resistance movements in various Nazis-occupied countries, which participation involved violence in many forms, including the ultimate violence of assassination. The witness of men like Dietrich Bonhoeffer and Kaj Munk is instructive in this regard. Needless to say, such extreme decisions are highly unlikely in any American context that we can now foresee. But they are important to cite to forestall the assumption that Christian action always means utilizing the respectable channels of democratic politics. We can rather think of Christian action as a continuum bounded on one end by democratic activity and by revolution on the other, with nonviolent resistance somewhere in between. Each situation calls for a decision geared to that situation. The situation of a Christian seeking slum clearance in Connecticut is different from that of a Christian seeking desegregation in Georgia. The situation of either is different from that of a Christian in present-day South Africa—or in 1956 in Hungary. What all the possibilities on this continuum of action have in common is their intention not only of alleviating but also of changing the social situation.

This essay, once more, is not the place for a critique of "social action" and of thinking about politics in American Protestantism.[3] We would state again, however, that Christian responsibility towards society will involve such action in many situations. No easy generalizations can be made as to what form this action must take. Each situation must be faced in its unique demands upon the Christian conscience. Within these limitations, there can be no doubt that Christian action is another relevant response to social reality, another valid form of social engagement. Yet the writer of this essay must confess a degree of pessimism about the efficacy of much that goes under the name of "social action" in our American situation. Sociological analysis shows rather clearly the political impotence of Protestantism as an institution in the community.[4] The previous discussion of the relationship of religion to the American political order shows how difficult it would be to mobilize the religious institution into the sort of activity that would overcome this impotence. Political action under religious auspices (especially Protestant ones) is notoriously inefficient. Furthermore, in many cases there are various secular groups within which Christians can express their political responsibility with much greater chance of success. Let it be said clearly once more that we would *not* want to denigrate the efforts of "social action" in the various forms it takes today in American Protestantism. We would only argue that, speaking realistically, it is difficult to imagine that these efforts will induce any significant changes in our social situation. By the very nature of its social functionality, the religious institution is one of the least likely agencies for the achievement of politically significant results. In certain situations one may feel constrained to try anyway. But if one remains close to empirical reality, one's enthusiasm is likely to be rather restrained.

Christian presence may be defined as the erection of Christian signs in the world. To the knowledge of this writer, the term derives (in its French form) from the Little Brothers of Jesus, a Roman Catholic order founded in 1933.[5] The order was founded under the inspiration of Father de Foucauld, a French priest who lived among the impoverished natives of the interior of Algeria, sharing their life in every respect except for his "total amity with Jesus."[6] The basic principle of the Little Brothers has remained this complete identification with the condition of the men among whom they live, earning their livelihood in the same way, deriving no funds from the outside, detached from the community only through their corporate worship and the adherence to their monastic discipline. Perhaps the extreme example of this practice of Christian presence is afforded by a small group of Little Sisters (the female branch of the order) who have voluntarily taken up residence in a South American prison for women, asking to be treated by the authorities in the same way as are the other prisoners, with the one exception of communicating without censorship with their superior. This radical concept of Christian presence, with some modifications, has been taken over by the Protestant Taizé Community, which has also felt a special responsibility to plant itself especially in situations of human conflict, misery, and degradation.

Even within French Catholicism this concept of Christian presence has been criticized as a form of quietism that avoids real involvement with social issues (for example, this has been the criticism of the worker-priests). For this reason it is important to stress that Christian presence, as we have defined it, cannot be a substitute either for Christian diaconate or for Christian action where these may be called for in terms of Christian responsibility for the world. However, there are situations in which Christians may have their hands tied in terms of any meaningful involvement in the events around them, in which they have no means to help and no power to act. In such cases the simple presence of those testifying to the fact that Christ continues to walk through the lives of all men, however hopeless or degraded or wicked their condition may be, is itself a relevant engagement with the world. Christian presence, in its social visibility, serves here as a sign of this continuing presence of Christ, the kenotic Christ who fully shares the human condition and all its suffering. In church history the situation of Orthodox Christians under Islam may serve as an example of this, where (at its best) the Orthodox community was nothing but such a sign, doing nothing, unable to do anything, except to witness in its liturgy and in its very being to the sovereignty of its Lord. The situation of Christians in Communist countries may resemble this state of affairs in some instances. Christian presence here may outwardly have the character of inaction and passivity. It may also include the deliberate refraining from any missionary activity. Yet this presence, even in silence, may constitute a meaningful engagement with social reality.

Again, the American situation is unlikely to provide many instances where Christian presence, in this sense, would be the only open course of social engagement. But against the taken-for-granted activism of American religion it is worth while to reiterate the validity, in some situations, of this symbolic witness. Also, as in other matters, there may be a legitimate division of labor here within the Christian community. It may be the task of some to be deacons and of others to be political activists and of still others to be silent witnesses to Christ's presence transcending and pre-empting any human efforts. Some of the best of Protestant preaching, even when struck with near-total blindness about the social reality in which it occurs, has sometimes been witness in this sense. To repeat: Such Christian presence cannot excuse us from serving human needs and meeting the active demands of Christian responsibility whenever this is possible. But the recollection of this possibility can help us to see that the Church is not just the sum total of its activities. The same possibility reminds us of the last line of retreat in situations where the powers of evil may appear to be overwhelming.

Christian dialogue may be defined as the attempt to engage the Christian faith in conversation with the world. This approach has been closely identified with the European laymen's movement and (taking this name from the laymen's institutes in Germany) has often been called the "Academy approach."[7] It has become the guiding light for various experiments within American Protestantism to make the churches more relevant to contemporary society. We shall look at this approach in some detail, since we would contend that it offers one of the best possibilities for social engagement and relevance in our own situation.

Perhaps the distinctiveness of this approach can be shown most easily by distinguishing it from Christian action, as defined above. Action depends upon a certain diagnosis of the situation that isolates certain facts or events as morally untenable and then proceeds to eliminate them or at least to modify them appreciably. Certainly there are many such facts and events in our society. But we would argue that these are the exception rather than the rule. Most of our social problems are so immensely complex that it is very difficult to locate evils in the first place, let alone to identify villains. Eberhard Mueller, the founder of the German "Academies," has called this phenomenon the "automation of evil." Our social problems today typically consist of the clash of highly organized interests, with well-meaning individuals caught on both sides in the logic and sometimes the ideology of their respective positions. Also, these problems are characterized by a high degree of incommunication between the groups and individuals participating in them. In many such instances, the classical approaches of "social action" fail even to get off the ground. One may not even know where one's action could begin. For example, most situations of industrial conflict in America today are far too complex for these old approaches. They involve highly complicated economic and political relationships, which it is very difficult to separate in terms of what is morally desirable or undesirable. In the early days of labor organization in America, when there were clear issues of economic exploitation and human indignity in almost every labor dispute, involvement in terms of "social action" may have been relatively easy for Christians. Today, more likely than not, these disputes do not involve economic issues at all. It is very hard for a consistent moralist to make decisions in disputes involving minutiae of work rules or job categories or in jurisdictional quarrels between rival unions. The temptation is close then simply to abandon such problems to the forces of the social situation, giving up the attempt to engage the situation in terms of Christian ethics at all. To yield to this temptation, however, is to say that the Christian faith is irrelevant to what are the crucial concerns of most men in industrial society. The great achievement of the "Academy movement" has been the demonstration that this is not so.

To say that there is incommunication between groups in modern society is not to say, of course, that these groups never talk to each other. They do so constantly—in negotiation, in debate, in propagandistic appeals to the public. Also, within each group there is much talking about its concerns, but this communication is either technical in character or consists of the construction of ideologies to defend the group against attacks from without. It is startling to reflect how few places there are in our society where people can come together and talk about the human problems of their social situations in an atmosphere of freedom, not as negotiators or propagandists or scientific researchers into these problems, but simply as human beings facing up to the moral reality of their lives. The "Academy movement" has regarded it as a Christian service to society to provide such places. It has furthermore assumed that the Christian faith, concerned as it is with real life, will show itself to be relevant when such free communication is allowed to occur.

In the European laymen's institutes, especially in Germany, this approach has become almost standardized in the years since the end of World War II. Yet the underlying principle is quite simple. The Christian institution that carries on this work invites distinctive groups of people to meet together to discuss some contemporary human or ethical problem. Very often these groups consist of people of the same vocation or different vocations involved in the same problem. In some places it has been the practice to involve from the beginning not only individuals but also organizations, on the sociologically valid assumption that it is only in organizations that individuals can bring to bear moral pressure in modern society. For example, if the problem in question is an industrial one, the invitation will go out to the organizations of management and labor concerned with this problem. Often individuals will be invited through the usual channels of these organizations. Almost always this invitation is extended to all regardless of religious affiliation or lack of affiliation. And it is made very clear that the Christian institution providing this place of dialogue is not interested in evangelism or in carrying out some project of political action or of telling people how they ought to run their lives. There is also a deliberate surrender of the classical ecclesiastical pretension to knowing the ultimate answer to every human problem under the sun. In many cases the role of the Christians in these dialogues is one of listening rather than speaking. The Church here does not present itself as an absolute moral authority that knows beforehand how the dialogue will end. Rather, it bears witness to its conscience by insisting that even the most complex economic problem has a moral and a human dimension. Christians are partners in the dialogue which seeks to discover this dimension. When people become convinced that these pre-suppositions are honestly held, that no Christian "soft sell" is being perpetrated on them, that they are really being taken seriously as human beings and are free to speak their mind, then it can happen that such dialogues become occasions of a profound sense of inner liberation from the bondages of society. In this experience the Christian faith shows itself to be relevant not only to the so-called spiritual side of men's lives but also to the men's common concerns in their jobs, in their private relation-ships, and in their political involvements.

Christians must enter into such dialogue with all their cards on the table. They must relinquish the idea that, in inviting both Christians and non-Christians to such communication, they will subject the latter to some subtle religious manipulation. They must not merely say, but honestly realize themselves, that they cannot know the answers to most of the problems arising in the dialogue. They must abandon the rhetorics of moral authority which too many contemporaries have learned to recognize as empty and pretentious verbiage. In many ways this approach represents a new posture of the Church, quite different from the kerygmatic posture so dear to many of our theologians. This posture has been called that of the listening Church. But it would be erroneous to regard this posture as a new expression of quietism. Listening in this context is a most active undertaking indeed. It means the concentration of every intellectual faculty on the tasks of understanding, of grasping the nuances of what is said, and of taking painstaking care that every human interest in the situation is heard and understood by all the participants. This process is far removed from the technology of "group dynamics." There is no intent of manipulating the psychology of the situation. The only technology involved has to do with providing the physical and social circumstances within which free communication can occur.

To illustrate this process, the example of a specific group might be taken. Let us take the example of secretaries employed in industry.[8] It is very likely that here is a group which has no organization at all, so that the approach will have to be made through individuals. The persons issuing the invitation will have to spend many hours with those individuals talking about the problems faced by this group. Various problem areas will open up in this way—the position of the secretary at the point of maximum cross fire from those above and below her in the organization; her own lack of organized representation; the general problems of boredom and meaninglessness in secretarial work; the peculiar role of the secretary as a woman in an essentially male world; the encroachments of work upon private life and the difficulties of creating one's own private sphere after the pressures of the workday—and possibly others peculiar to the group in question and quite unexpected in the beginning. It is only after some of these problems have been located in many personal conversations that anything resembling a program can be constructed. Again, this may take different forms— weekend conferences in some quiet place, seminars or discussion groups meeting at varying frequencies, lunch-hour meetings in or near the plant. Just as it is important not to approach the group with a definite program in mind, it is important that one has no inflexible procedure to recommend (such as, for instance, a firm belief in "retreat"-type conferences or in the ultimate efficacy of small groups). Also, there can be no rule about the participation of those (be they clergymen or not) who initiate the program. There may be groups where their participation should be minimal and should not go significantly beyond the task of arranging the externals of the meetings—as in groups that are highly articulate or where strongly conflicting interests are involved. On other occasions a more active leadership in the conversations themselves may be called for—as in groups not used to disciplined discussion or in groups whose discussion might degenerate into mutual self-congratulation. All these questions can be decided upon only in the context of the particular communication process that one intends to set in motion. The only general rule is that of meticulous respect for persons and the only general prohibition is against any form of manipulation. This also means that the question must be left open as to the point at which one will feel free to speak in terms of the Christian faith or whether such a point is reached at all in the particular group. It must also be left open (that means left to the group itself) whether there is to be any consequence to the conversations in terms of some kind of action or wider publicity. In many cases no results can be pointed to other than the clarification of issues within the group itself. Yet it must be stressed that this is no mean result amid the incommunication of modern society.

While the "Academy approach" has been most developed in the churches of western Europe, it is increasingly felt by many to be of great significance in the American situation as well, a situation similar in many ways to that across the Atlantic. We would leave open the question as to the possibilities of this approach outside the orbit of what has, with increasing justification, been called the north-Atlantic civilization (although we may mention that similar ventures are under way in a number of so-called "Younger Churches" in Asia and Africa). We would contend again that it appears as one of the most hopeful avenues of social engagement within that orbit. In the American situation, with its competitive denominational system, we would also contend that this approach must almost inevitably take on an ecumenical character. And there are already hopeful signs of what such an approach can accomplish. The work of the Department of the Church and Economic Life of the National Council of Churches in its vocational conferences across the country has shown what can be done on this level of the churches' concern for society. The work of the Detroit Industrial Mission may serve as an illustration of an ongoing Christian dialogue with the economic forces in one metropolitan area. The imaginative experiments of the Christian Faith and Life Community at the University of Texas have become a model for a new Christian engagement with the academic world. The Institute of Church and Community at the Hartford Seminary has been trying to develop an "Academy approach" from the base of an ecumenical theological seminary, seeking to relate the intellectual resources of such an institution to the Christian engagement with society and, in turn, to feed back into the seminary curriculum the insights gained in this approach.[9] In these cases Christian dialogue is undertaken by agencies specially created for this purpose on levels beyond those of local churches. This does not mean, however, that this form of social engagement has no possibilities on the local level. Of this, however, we shall have more to say in the next chapter.

If one were to seek a key concept to relate this possibility of Christian dialogue to our sociological analysis of American religion, that concept might be that of "de-ideologizing" (with due apologies to the much-persecuted English language). We have seen the place of ideology in our religious institution. Ideology occupies a similarly central place in the existence of other institutions as well, especially in the occupational world. It is a sociological commonplace that social groups manufacture convenient illusions that rationalize and ratify their roles in society. The clergy have no monopoly on this. It is true of physicians, advertisers, public-relations experts, labor-union officials—and even social scientists. "De-ideologizing" means the process of radically honest thinking and communicating by which these systematic illusions are breached. It denotes the experience in which social groups come to face the reality of their situation. Sometimes such an experience can be quite dramatic—as in the case of an advertising copywriter first grasping in his guts the moral significance of manipulation or of a physician understanding in the same way the human meaning of the differential life expectancy of different social classes. But "de-ideologizing" can occur on Christian ground only if the Church is willing to look at itself in the same ruthlessly honest way. In helping others to look at themselves honestly, the Church will find that it must do the same in terms of its own social reality. What is possible here is a "vicious circle" of truth. That is, the liberators find themselves liberated. In this possibility lies the great moral significance of the sort of unmasking that occurs when Christian dialogue is carried on with passion.

Despite the writer's inclinations, this discussion of Christian dialogue has been brief or it would have burst the framework of this essay. However, there still remains one question that ought to be touched: Why should this task of communication and "de-ideologizing" be the particular concern of the churches? Or, stated differently, could this not be done just as well by secular institutions? One may point out here that similar questions can be raised about diaconal service and "social action" carried on by churches. And the most obvious answer is the same as the one that could have been given some one hundred years ago when Christians were asked why they went out to build hospitals in the jungles of Africa: There was no one else doing this. We can say today that almost nobody is doing what has been described in the preceding paragraphs and that, consequently, Christians simply have an opportunity here to use their imagination in loving their neighbors. At some future date the situation might be different. But while this answer is valid, there is a deeper answer that is possible. Social reality being what it is, any process of facing one's own situation in society involves an encounter with guilt. Indeed, very often the entire enterprise of ideology is motivated by an avoidance of guilt. Thus, "de-ideologizing" has a very close relationship to what Christians mean by conversion—and by justification by faith. This does not mean at all that Christians have some prerogative in the search for truth. But they have more to offer to the seeker than a "terrible freedom." The Christian faith not only unmasks guilt but also is capable of speaking of grace. In other words, the Christian faith allows men to face their guilt more honestly because it insists that guilt is not the last word of the human morality play. Finally (and this is most important in the last resort) the Christian faith looks at human existence and human society under the aspect of redemption. This means that it can afford to take the world less seriously than it takes itself. Christian debunking is therefore free from the bitterness and humorlessness that is often the trademark of the professional radical.[10]

What has been said in this chapter should at least make quite clear that when we speak of the task of disestablishment we are not suggesting some sort of social disaffiliation. On the contrary! As Christians free themselves from the bondage of the taken-for-granted religious establishment, they become free to engage society at all its focal points. Disestablishment is the very opposite of a retreat into a Christian ghetto. It is rather the presupposition to a fully contemporary and fully conscious Christian mission in modern society. All the dimensions of this social engagement are not yet apparent. There are difficulties not only of the social forces in our situation but also of personal doubts and intellectual perplexities. But Christian mission has never been without risks. Any act of faith implies a deliberate choice of risk.

10

The Problem of New Forms

A problem that was touched upon in the preceding chapter is increasingly occupying the attention of those concerned with the social engagement of Christians. This is the problem of new forms of the Church in modern society, forms that may be called for if the Church is to fulfil its mission in that society. One important facet of the same problem is obviously the relationship of these new forms, whatever they may be, to the old forms now institutionalized in our religious life—denominations, interdenominational agencies, local congregations, and so on. The problem evidently has its theological as well as sociological sides. Theologically, the problem raises various questions of ecclesiology. These, however reluctantly, we cannot follow up within the confines of this essay. But we must look at the sociological aspects of the problem, since they relate crucially to what we have said before about the tasks facing Christians in the American situation.

In the minds of most people the problem comes to a focus (and rightly so) in the consideration of the local congregation. For American Protestantism this is the form of religious organization to which most Christians relate directly. Clergy and clericalized laymen may be more interested at times in the wider organizational patterns. But for most lay Christians the form of the Church that means anything to them personally is their own local congregation. At the most they will also include in their personal frame of reference the relations of this congregation with other local congregations in the same community. The problem of new forms of the Church and their relationship to the old forms thus naturally centers on the problem of the local congregation and its social character and potentiality for mission in modern society. Both in Europe and in this country there has developed a considerable body of literature concerned with the "revitalization" of the local congregation (or of the parish, depending on the particular denominational parlance) as the most important task facing Christians today.[1]

This literature frequently shows a keen awareness of the changing social circumstances of our contemporary situation. It calls for new approaches, sometimes daring ones. Yet it also is characterized by an essential conservatism concerning the institutional forms of religion. Since most of this literature is written by clergy—that means by people whose social existence is grounded in the religious institution—this is perhaps only natural. We would contend, however, that this conservative bias begs some important questions. We might take as an example the following passage from Martin Marty's recent book on American religion (a book which, let it be said clearly, is a valuable contribution to our understanding):

In discussing the forms through which theological insights might shape American religious life, we shall be dealing in a positive way with institutions. For my own part, I must view "anti-institutionalism" as a cheap solution and emphatically disagree with its proponents. Too often the critics of contemporary religion join in massive assault on congregation, seminary or denomination. New iconoclasts, they would shatter the forms that centuries have developed and that the good sense of Christian people has brought to maturity. Misapplying a theorem of Henri Bergson's these iconoclasts assume that religious ferment must always harden and crystallize in its second generation.

The historian and the reporter, however, must turn with some hope to institutions. And I for one believe that *we already possess the institutions we need to undertake the religious task set before America today.*[2]

This kind of conservatism has all the appeal of moderation and common sense—characteristics which the writer of this essay also finds attractive. Unfortunately, such conservatism also tends to underestimate the strength of the social forces in the situation. Despite all its readiness to suggest new departures within the institution, it takes the over-all institutional framework for granted. This is intellectually dangerous, because a clear perception of any social institution demands the readiness, at least in principle, to take nothing for granted. It might then happen that one ultimately arrives at a conservative position at the conclusion of such a sociological adaptation of the Cartesian method of doubt. But one cannot start out from such a position and hope to see the situation clearly. As to the passage given here as an example, it is not enough to call the radical questioning of our religious institutions "cheap" or to call the questioners "iconoclasts." The same charge could be (and indeed was) made against the prophetic critique of the Israelite cultus and of the Pauline critique of Judaism, and virtually the same words could have been used by Erasmus in his rejection of the Lutheran Reformation. The assumption that religion hardens in institutional forms is not a misunderstanding of Henri Bergson but is possibly the most important consequence of the sociology of religion, coming into sharp focus in Max Weber's work on the "routinization of charisma." As to whether we already possess the institutions to fulfil the Christian mission in American society, that precisely is the question to be decided: it cannot be the *a priori* from which to start our investigation.

It should be reiterated that much that is true and relevant can be said from such a conservative position, as, indeed, has been done by Martin Marty. Furthermore, the writer of this essay can readily agree with much that is said in this view. The same could be admitted with regard to such recent statements on the mission of the Church in America as those of George Webber[3] or Robert Spike.[4] We would readily agree with Webber that the Christian community should be a divine "colony" in the world and with Spike that there is bondage to the safety of American religion. We must also ask, however, in what way the present institutional patterns of American religion help or hinder becoming such a "colony," help or hinder the exodus from safety that is called for. As has been said before, we cannot be satisfied with the neo-orthodox reiteration that the Christian faith always expresses itself in *koinonia* and then participate in the intellectual *salto mortale* that identifies this *koinonia* with the Methodist or Lutheran church around the corner, or with the Methodist or Lutheran denominational organization, or even with the Methodist or Lutheran historical tradition. On the contrary, the question that concerns us is precisely in what way Methodism or Lutheranism or any other social-historical entity of this kind can be identified with the *koinonia* that waits upon its risen Lord. We would contend once more that the anti-empirical animus of neo-orthodoxy (however justified it may have been some decades ago as a reaction to the moralism and psychologism of theological liberalism) has done us a bad turn in this question. What can happen here with frightening ease is that ecclesiology becomes an escape from social reality—the reality of the world as much as the reality of the religious institution. One then constructs an ecclesiological structure—perhaps one that is theologically impeccable—and then one lives in the illusion that this structure can be found in the empirical churches in which one worships and (not to be forgotten!) which often pay one's salary.

Our quarrel here is not with this or that doctrine of the Church. For the moment we would leave this question aside. What we have to say here can be relevant to the Anglo-Catholic as well as the Unitarian. Ecclesiology can go on in any direction of which the theological imagination is capable. Our immediate interest in it begins at the point where it impinges on empirical data. And at this point we must hold again that, if our sociological analysis of American religion is correct, the social forces in our situation militate against any of the tasks that are commonly presented to us as Christian imperatives. These social forces must be taken seriously; otherwise, theological thinking becomes ideology and theological existence becomes bad faith.

Our contention of the nature of the social forces in our situation can easily be illustrated in terms that can be understood by anyone familiar with the everyday reality of American Protestantism. Let us imagine, for the sake of the argument, that a typical middle-class local congregation would really want to start a "colony" of God in the midst of the world, to use Webber's phrase once more—or, rather, to be more accurate, that a group within such a congregation would have this intention. Almost immediately a set of pressures would be set loose, all militating against the realization of the project. Some of these pressures are local, some involve the larger religious organizations.

The most obvious pressures are economic.[5] These manifest themselves in both local and organizational expectations. The economic pressures (constantly rising as a result of inflation) prescribe quite rigidly what the basic course is to be that any local congregation ought to take. The organization will recognize that there are some areas (which, one feels, ought to be included in the "coverage" of the denomination) that will remain financial drains for the foreseeable future. The inner city is commonly one of these areas. Within the organization the program for these areas is frequently segregated within the budget under such headings as "home missions" or "marginal ministries." Economic logic dictates the extent to which the organization can afford such luxuries. As to the bulk of local churches within the organization, a different logic operates in a taken-for-granted way. New churches are started in areas with a "high potential," that is, areas in which there is a population likely to be interested in affiliating with the denomination in question and in which there are high enough economic resources to permit the hope that the church will be self-supporting in a reasonable time. More and more, the decision to go into a new area is based on careful research into the social and economic characteristics of the area in question. The causality behind this care is, once more, economic rather than religious. It is the same causality that underlies market research carried on by commercial enterprises—mainly the inflationary spiral behind the cost of initial outlay and ongoing maintenance. Once a church has been established, certain stages in its development are taken for granted. Each of these stages releases new economic pressures.

Both local opinion (including that of the new membership) and the organization expect the church to have its own building at the earliest possible date. This means that, from the beginning, the activities of the "missionary" minister have a double character—that of the enlistment of as many members as possible and that of the engagement of as much money as possible in the new ecclesiastical enterprise. The development of the new congregation can thus be represented statistically in terms of two indices, a demographic and a fiscal one—and, of course, it is thus that it is looked upon by the organization as the latter maps out its general strategy. In terms of the organizational problems in this age of inflation it is perhaps enough to point out that, at the time of writing, about one hundred million dollars are being spent monthly in this country on the construction of new churches.[6] In terms of the local congregation, even at minimal levels of expenditure, tens of thousands of dollars figure almost at once in a budget that is geared to a building campaign. It is easy to see what this means to a local congregation in which there is some concern for the quality as well as the quantity of membership. Under whatever theological rationalization, the primary imperative in this situation is to live up to the statistical expectations. Once the building is there, of course, there are the continuing pressures of mortgage payments and maintenance expenses, not to speak of the cost of the staff needed to carry on the kind of program demanded by the membership in the typical congregation.

As a result, there emerges a fairly clear image of what "success" means in the local congregation. In brief, "success" means an expanding membership, an expanding budget, and an expanding program. We may recall here what was said earlier in this essay on American values, specifically on the success-orientation of American culture, to see that this pattern is well in accord with the secular culture in general. We may also emphasize the self-perpetuating character of this pattern. The establishment of new churches means, from the start, the setting in motion of a large economic apparatus. Once established, the apparatus must be maintained. Even if there were no other considerations, economic considerations alone would dictate this. The more expensive such an operation becomes in our inflationary economy, the more compelling is the logic that forces it into a preconceived direction. Yet, in most cases, introspective considerations hardly arise, for everyone shares the cultural values and expectations that take the operation for granted.

For the organization to which the local congregation belongs, political as well as economic pressures are important. It should be emphasized that this is true regardless of "polity." It would be a grave error to assume that only those denominations that adhere to a conception of a strong ecclesiastical structure (such as Episcopalians or Methodists) face these political pressures. Even denominations with an avowed "polity" of extreme decentralization and local autonomy face the same pressures.[7] The decisive variable here is not "polity" but degree of bureaucratization. The latter, we dare say, is pretty much the same in our middle-class denominations. These political pressures originate both within the organization and from its relations with competing organizations. Within the organization there is the usual phenomenon of "Parkinson's law." Each board, commission, or committee seeks to perpetuate itself, to enlarge its importance within the total organization, and to justify its budget. These goals require "success" in the activities allocated to the agency in question within the organizational charts. To achieve these goals and thus to allay the pressures on the agency within the organization, it becomes necessary to exert pressure oneself —in this case, pressure on the local congregation. This can happen in a variety of ways, ranging from personal persuasion to the withholding or granting of funds at the agency's disposal. The end result of these pressures is to direct the local branches of the organization into the desired channels of action. However, pressures also originate in the "external relations" of the organization. These deserve some special attention, since they illustrate a particularly ironic consequence of "ecumenicity."

The operations of middle-class, "central-core" denominations in American Protestantism, especially those concerned with "church extension," are today commonly undertaken in consultation and negotiation with other denominations. This consulting process, once called "comity" but now more commonly called "planning," is one of the most important functions of local and regional councils of churches. These ecumenical agencies operate politically in much the same way as the local and regional organs of the AFL-CIO operate in jurisdictional disputes between rival labor unions. And, not surprisingly, very similar frictions arise. Thus, the "planning" agency in question will normally allocate the new area to a specific denomination—say, the Presbyterians. But if the area in question is a "high-potential" one, we can be sure that, say, the Methodists and the Baptists will be somewhat annoyed by this decision. In such cases, it is sometimes rather difficult to arrive at rules of equity that satisfy everybody. We can then also be sure that the Methodists and the Baptists are going to watch rather closely what the Presbyterians are going to do with the plum that has thus been placed in their lap. The Presbyterians, knowing this all too well, will have to justify the allocation made to them by the "planning" agency. All of this adds up to a new spiral of pressures, this time political rather than economic ones. And, as in the case of the economic pressures, these pressures are all in the direction of "success," as this term can be expressed in statistical evidence.

Ironically (in a religion that has emphasized the priesthood of all believers) these pressures all come together in the life of one person—the minister. For the others, there are pressures that touch them more or less tangentially, depending upon the degree of their religious commitment. For him, these pressures touch not only upon his central convictions but also upon his professional self-image, his career, and the economic base of his existence (not to mention that of his family!). All the economic and political pressures towards "success" come to a focus in the minister's role, powerfully coercing him to be "successful" himself. Whether the minister's denomination has an episcopal or a congregational "polity," his career chances can be estimated in terms of this notion of what he ought to be. The large churches and the well-paying appointments will normally go to the "successful." The rest will have to be satisfied with what their organizational superiors will often refer to as "challenging situations." When one adds to this the fact that to many if not most ministers there is no real conflict here at all, since they themselves share the values and aspirations that go with these pressures, one may understand the full weight of what happens here. Unless the evidence on human motives and actions accumulated by social psychology since William James can be dismissed out of hand, we should certainly not be surprised if our ministers will generally become what the social situation expects of them—that is, become "successful," or, at the very least, strive towards this goal. Christian laymen, who (like the writer of this essay) find the pretensions, pathos, and paraphernalia of the ministerial role humanly disagreeable, may have a little difficulty at times in working up much sympathy for this clerical predicament. But if one has had the opportunity to listen when ministers talk among themselves, at private gatherings or in the back rooms of ecclesiastical assemblages, one cannot help but be touched by the suffering (sometimes barely admitted) that this role entails. To use the terms coined by Erving Goffman, the discrepancy between the minister's "front-stage" poise and his "back-stage" disenchantment then strikes one with the force of shock. One may also realize then the moral weakness of the layman's tendency to put the onus of the Church's failures on this one group. If only because of the economic and political realities of our church life, ministers will tend to be what we expect them to be. Consequently, we cannot use their lack of leadership as an alibi for our own sub-Christian expectations.

All the same, as we look at these various pressures on the local congregation and its personnel, it is rather difficult to come out with the sort of optimistic evaluation that the afore-mentioned conservative position entails. Christians will not want to pre-empt the operations of grace. God can work miracles even in the valley of dead bones. Christian responsibility, however, cannot be exhausted in a waiting upon miracles. It must involve calculation within an economy of effort. If we thus calculate, taking into full account the social realities, we arrive at a pessimistic view of the efforts to "revitalize" the local congregation. Where such attempts have been successful, the congregations in question were typically on the verge of economic bankruptcy—in the Protestant diaspora situation in the inner city, in areas of rapid change in the racial constituency of the population, or in overchurched and underpopulated rural areas. We would certainly not want to disparage these efforts, which in most cases were a responsible Christian reaction to these particular circumstances. But the typical situation of American Protestantism is not in East Harlem but in Westchester County. It is with regard to this typical local congregation that we must admit to pessimism.

What we are suggesting is quite simple. The sharp edge of the Christian engagement with the modern world is not likely to be in the parish. We might possibly make some hopeful concessions about the potentialities of the local congregation in the task of personal conversion and of the accustomed church institutions in the task of theological construction. But even this becomes hard to do when we think about the task of social engagement, especially in the active varieties that we discussed in the preceding chapter. We would contend that these will have to occur in "supraparochial" settings, some of them to be created as new forms of the Church in the modern world.

The work of the laymen's institutes, the industrial missions, and other gatherings of Christians "outside the walls" can give us valuable indications of the shapes that may be in the making here. It should be noticed, however, that none of these enterprises developed out of a blueprint concerning a reorganization of the Church in modern society. There was a burning need for service and Christians answered this need. In many cases, reflection about the full meaning of what was happening came only long afterwards, and even then it frequently led to more puzzlement. This should suggest that the ultimate shape of the Church cannot be the subject of planning. What we must plan is our own response to our very own situations. In these situations we must do what we think we have to do. The final consequences of our actions cannot be foreseen. This is why the discussion of the relationship of old and new forms of the Church, as soon as one gets beyond immediate practical questions, often takes on a strange character of unreality.

If we want to stay clear of such ecclesiological utopianism, there are still a few things that can be said very practically. In terms of local churches in our communities, the most fruitful direction in which we can think is that of the "larger parish" concept. It is very much to be regretted (though very understandable sociologically) that this concept usually appears on the scene at the point where the roof threatens to fall in— typically, in the inner city or in underprivileged rural areas.

The importance of the concept, however, is in the possibility that it raises for ecumenical co-operation in the "supraparochial" tasks of the Christian community without infringing on the jealously guarded political, theological, and liturgical peculiarities of the several denominations represented in the area. Perhaps a better name for the kind of concept we have in mind would be that of "ecumenical parish." It goes without saying that such a concept demands a considerable degree of reorientation on the part of local congregations—but still less so than is usually called for by the various plans to convert the local congregation itself into a dynamic instrument of engagement with the world. Perhaps the most difficult rethinking called for here is that of considering the presence of the Church in any one place as an ecumenical one. That is, it means to think of *all* the Christians in the community as the "Church in Middletown" or the "Church on the Upper West Side" or perhaps even the "Church in the Metropolitan Area." It further means that each local congregation must abandon its favorite prima-donna illusions about its capacities to make an impact upon the community. The various active tasks of social engagement— Christian diaconate, Christian action, and Christian dialogue— will then be understood as ecumenical tasks, concerns of the entire Christian "parish" in the community. It will be the "ecumenical parish" as a whole that will stand out as a signal of Christian presence in the community. Then, insofar as Christians gathered "outside the walls" to carry on their mission in the world relate themselves to the religious institution, they will do so in ecumenical rather than parochial terms. As happens with every concerted effort in modern society, the realization of such a concept will entail a certain amount of organization. But it must be stressed once more that organization is not the key to the problem. Instead, the realization requires a new way of thinking and acting as a Christian in the American situation. The organizational forms that will then become necessary are in the nature of *adiaphora,* subject to the rationale and the practicalities of specific cases.

Although we come dangerously close to dreaming about Spanish castles if we think beyond this point, it may be permissible to speculate that such a new way of thinking might have consequences beyond the social engagement that concerns us most at the moment. Christians of different denominational camps have frequently come closer to each other in the undertaking of common tasks than in the course of theological disputations (which are often meaningless to the layman). This is not to denigrate the important theological aspects of ecumenical encounter, but simply to suggest that a new approach to the task of social engagement may also have results that go beyond the latter. Thus, it might even be possible that American Protestants subject to a Christian critique the present multiplication of church edifices, with the horrendous economic and spiritual costs of this building boom. Perhaps a way might be found for different Christian groups to worship in the same building at different hours. Perhaps eventually it might even be possible to build churches that express the ecumenical presence in the community with the finest resources of contemporary architecture, instead of the aesthetic monstrosities that now litter the map and that owe their character to the economic exigencies of our present taken-for-granted assumptions about our church life.

Sociologists will very naturally be pessimistic about the possibilities of deliberate social change. This pessimism will increase if the situation at hand concerns an institution that is well established in its present modes of operation. The principle of economy of effort takes on special importance in such a perspective. But if there is anything that makes for optimism concerning the hesitant proposals of the preceding paragraphs, it is the economic aspects of these proposals. Most projects of social reform are tremendously expensive. What we have suggested here is not. In fact, if the concept of the "ecumenical parish" became a realistic possibility in our situation, there could occur a considerable degree of rationalization in the surrealistic fiscal structure of our religious organizations. We are pessimistic enough about human nature to be able to be optimistic about possibilities that save money. The same pessimism allows us a measure of optimism about changes that do not demand a total reordering of the institution in question.

As far as the local congregation is concerned, our considerations lead us to a somewhat paradoxical conclusion. We find ourselves far more radical than most in negatively estimating the potentialities of the institution. At the same time, we would be more conservative than most in terms of what we would want to do with the institution. The clue to the paradox, of course, is our contention that the most urgent tasks before us can be dealt with outside the institution and, at least in certain cases, with little reference to it. The local congregation can then be left to what it has always done and perhaps will always do in the future—liturgy, preaching, the administration of the sacraments, and whatever educational activities seem plausible to those concerned. Essential tasks of the Christian mission in our society can then be undertaken (radically, if need be) outside the local congregation.

Such a conclusion may sound a little like an injunction to let the dead bury their dead. This is not our intention. One might even raise the question of whether some of those who would radically transform the local congregation are quite fair to many in it. For example, there are many of the aged and the sick and the emotionally crippled in our congregations to whom these radical calls for institutional revolution can mean nothing but a threat to whatever spiritual solace the congregation has been able to give them. There is every reason to speak of the vocation of Christians in industrial society, for instance. But there are some Christians whose one vocation remains to suffer and to face death in faith. It is certainly no minor accomplishment if a local congregation provides the communal support for such a vocation. Such accomplishment is unspectacular and very unrevolutionary, but it is enough to forbid the assumption that *only* in radical new forms can the Church perform a witness.

During a recent visit to this country, Hans-Ruedi Weber of the World Council of Churches expressed his conviction that for quite some time we shall have to restrain our craving for neat solutions and that different forms of Christian endeavor will continue to exist side by side without any easy ways of combining them in over-all strategies.[8] We would strongly share this view. As there were different *charismata* in the early Church, so there may have to be a division of labor in the Church's mission in modern society. We have already commented on the dubious attitude that would regard the minister as a "vicarious Christian" and push on him the burden of the questions raised in this essay. It is also dubious (and unrealistic to boot) to expect that the imperatives of one situation can be translated into a program for the Church everywhere. So it is quite possible to concede that for some Christians the local congregation may continue to be the primary locale for the expression of their faith. For others it will be elsewhere. For the churches, as complex social organizations, this means a great deal of flexibility in their thinking about the mission before them. The meaning for the individual we shall look at in our concluding remarks.

V

Postscript on Commitment

A common technique of preachers and other religious functionaries is to throw the most shocking questions at their audience
and then to neutralize their effect carefully by answering them
within the framework demanded by their context. When one
uses such a technique one gives the appearance of "really facing
up to the questions." In reality one does nothing of the kind
because, on the contrary, the sting is taken out of the questions
by asking them in the particular context that already takes the
answers for granted. After the little exercise, the audience is
all the better insulated against doubt. Imagine that you find
yourself in church on a Sunday morning and that, after the
hymns have been sung and the announcements have been made
and the congregation has settled down for the sermon, the
preacher sweeps back his robe and begins with the question,
"Can one still be a Christian today?" For one brief moment
(perhaps a moment of wild hope) the thought may enter your
mind that he will answer "no," take off his robe, and walk out
of the church never to come back! Naturally you will dismiss
such a thought immediately. And the preacher will do nothing
of the sort. Whatever he says in his sermon, he will not
jeopardize what remains of the ceremony—another hymn, another prayer, the collection, and the smiling handshake at the
door. Since you know this from the beginning, the question with
which he has opened his sermon cannot be taken seriously.
In other words, the outcome of the exercise is "fixed."
    The argument of this essay would be characterized by the

same sort of bad faith if it now came to a conclusion by urging the reader to go out and get busy in the religious organization of his choice. Anyone who has followed the argument to this point will readily see that such a conclusion could not be arrived at honestly. It would render innocuous the entire critique that has been undertaken. It would insult both the intelligence and the integrity of the reader. If this is to be avoided, our conclusion must be less neat—and more controversial.

This essay is addressed primarily to Christians rather than to those looking at the Christian faith from the outside. We assume, then, that we are addressing those to whom Christian commitment is at least a live option. It was on this assumption that we discussed the tasks facing Christian commitment in our situation —tasks of personal conversion, of honest intellectual search, and of engagement with social reality. We would contend once more that these tasks are Christian imperatives in our situation, imperatives that concern all of us who would seek to follow Christ. An altogether different question is the way in which these tasks relate to the ongoing business of the religious institution.

In discussing the problems and possibilities of the Protestant churches in America, we have tried very hard to see the situation sharply and not to be carried away by the *élan* of extreme formulations. Especially in the last chapter we have discussed various new avenues that the churches might explore, and we have been careful to point out the continuing validity of some of the old ones. We have certainly not suggested and would explicitly reject here the notion that Christian commitment in our situation demands a withdrawal from organized religion. But at the same time we cannot see our way to the opposite position, which would say that Christian commitment, now and presumably always, demands full adherence to the empirical entities we call churches in everyday language. We especially cannot see this in our situation in mid-century America.

We have previously discussed the possibility of a division of labor in the field of Christian engagement with the world. Different people might do different things, with no over-all plan available for everybody. We would now suggest that this possibility might even go farther than that. To put this in the form of a simple proposition: *Involvement with organized religion is a Christian vocation.*

The proposition calls for further explication. It does not really make sense to say that loving one's neighbor is a Christian vocation. Every Christian is commanded to love his neighbor. But not every Christian is called to do so as, say, a nurse. To be a nurse, consequently, is a Christian vocation, in the sense of being the calling in which some Christians will seek to express their commitment. By the same token, other Christians are not so called and will feel free to walk on other roads. The above proposition intends to be understood in the same way.

Obviously such a viewpoint raises serious theological questions, specifically questions concerning a doctrine of the Church. But this essay is not the place to deal with these. It might be pointed out, however, that theology must develop not only a doctrine of the Church but also a doctrine of the churches. In other words, ecclesiology must contain empirical reality in its perspective. It is not enough, therefore, to say that the Christian faith must always express itself in the community of the Church (a statement with which we would tend to agree). One must also point out in what way this community relates to the institutions that confront us in society. At this point, theology often leaves us in the lurch. Nor does our proposition seek to deny that the Church will take on institutional forms in history and that it is utopian to expect these forms to meet an ideal constructed by ecclesiology. We know all this. We can look upon the Church as an army moving through time, an *Ecclesia militans* that, by the very token of its militancy, shares in the ambiguities and the imperfections of all human events. But if we recognize the legitimacy of this army, we can still admit that some may be called to be francs-tireurs outside its ranks. Historical situations will vary in the demands they make both upon the regular troops and upon the irregulars freely roaming the countryside. Historical situations will always present new vocations to the Christian and sometimes will render impossible the ones he would most like to follow.

It is very dangerous to speak of "the Biblical witness" as if it were a consistent structure of thought applying to all human situations. There are many Biblical witnesses and we are compelled to choose between them. In terms of our considerations here, it will obviously make a great difference whether we select as our witness the prophets or the priestly code, the Pauline literature or the pastoral epistles. We can make our choice only through a passionate desire to obey God in our own situation and through a sensitive listening to the demands of this situation. We cannot select our proof texts and then sit on them without further worry. There are different texts for different times. Thus, it is quite possible that "the Biblical witness" for times of persecution may lie in those texts that stress the adherence of the Christian to the visible, social symbols of his faith. A proposition such as *"Extra Ecclesia nulla salus"* has one significance when Christians are dying in the arena and quite another when Christians are spectators in the stalls. For example, adherence to the church in Rome might indeed have been a condition of salvation during the persecution of Diocletian. But adherence to the church in Spain might have been a seal of damnation in the days of Torquemada—and, for some, during the days of the Spanish Civil War, when Christian priests blessed the weapons of the fascist firing squads. The text for the one situation might recall that Yahweh delights in the worship of Jerusalem, for the other that He spits upon the altars of Samaria.

Our American situation is different from fourth-century Rome and different from fifteenth-century Spain. However, even if our religious establishment is not one that rests on a foundation of violence, its very existence, as we have tried to analyze it, gives us a prejudice for the prophetic rather than the priestly witnesses. And so, if we are once more to select a saying of Jesus as a guide for our considerations, we would suggest a text from the Sermon on the Mount: "Not every one who says to me, 'Lord, Lord,' shall enter the kingdom of heaven, but he who does the will of my Father who is in heaven" (Matthew 7:21).

Those of us coming from liturgical churches may feel a particular chill when we associate this text with the *Kyrie* of our common worship. Nor is it impossible that this liturgical implication was present in the original intention of the text. Be this as it may, the picture of the liturgy is suggestive here. The churches are essentially the places of liturgy. And this is as it should be. But liturgy is not the key to the kingdom of Christ. The key is obedience in faith and action. As Dietrich Bonhoeffer once put it during the Nazi era, only he who cries out for the Jews has the right to sing Gregorian chants. In the context of the Sermon on the Mount, our passage follows Jesus' strong warning against false prophets, who may be recognized as such by their fruits. There are situations in which the *Kyrie,* pronounced in beautiful cathedrals surrounded by festering slums, may itself be such a sign of recognition of false prophecy. It is this variety of Biblical witness that is needed especially in times of social and religious security—times that call for dissonant voices to hurl the word of God's anger against the cows of Bashan. This is why we would choose this particular text for our American religious establishment.

In this choice we find both warning and comfort. The warning puts in question many of our taken-for-granted assumptions. It shows up the idolatry that would limit the presence of Christ to the ecclesiastical circles that we ourselves have drawn. It debunks the moral myopia that understands Christian commitment in terms of financial contributions and organizational activity, that seeks to grasp the Christian life in statistical indices, and that perceives a national recession in terms of a crisis in the church extension budget. It also puts in question the entire institutional logic which provides the illusion that the act of church affiliation is in itself an act of faith in Jesus Christ. This moral judgment gives an answer to the *Kyrie* rising upwards from countless pseudo-Gothic edifices across the land—"You are not my people and I am not your God" (Hosea 1:9).

At the same time, there is a comfort in this text. It liberates us from the bondage of the institutional logic. It gives us the reassurance that any effort of genuine obedience to the will of God carries with it a promise of redemption. It opens up the possibility of vocation where before there was only the burden of servitude. We then are no longer imprisoned in the "solemn assemblies" (Amos 5:21) of our religious establishment and, by that same token, we become free to seek that justice that rolls "down like waters" (Amos 5:24). Our eyes become opened to the immense horizons of the world and to the consciousness of Christ's presence on all possible horizons and in the furthest corners of the world. We may then find that the security of the establishment and its "O.K. world" was a very cheap price to pay for the freedom that is God's will for men.

We have been anxious to defend as strongly as possible that kind of Christian vocation that finds its way outside the social forms of the establishment. This is very important because our cultural climate makes the recognition of such a vocation very difficult. Let there be no uncertainty as to what we are saying: we are suggesting that Christians may freely choose *not* to become members of local congregations, *not* to identify themselves with a denomination, *not* to join the weekly traffic jam of the religious rush hour on Sunday morning. We are suggesting that these decisions might be directly grounded in the Christian faith as it seeks to relate itself to our situation. And we are contending that such decisions might be the legitimate exercise of a Christian vocation in our time.

However, having made this point as emphatically as we were able, we would not arrest ourselves there. We would avoid fixation in a radical posture just as much as fixation in an ecclesiastical one. We would once more emphasize the liberty and openness implicit in the concept of vocation. And we would again stress the possibilities of Christian service that may be found within both old and new forms of the empirical churches. Finally, we would address our concluding remarks to *both* vocations—

the one inside and the one outside the walls of the sanctuaries in which the *Kyrie* is sung.

In our preface we have stressed the importance for Christians of lucid, fearless perception of social reality. We would go further now and stress not only independence of thinking but also rebelliousness of attitude. Our time has had its share of organization men. Now it needs insurrectionary spirits, adventurers, rebels. And it needs—very badly indeed—Christian rebels. If rebellion against the inertia and indolence of our cultural climate carries with it a certain amount of uncouthness and occasionally unfairness to what is best in our traditions, this is a minor consideration. We have had enough soft-spoken manners in the Christian community. We now need loudmouthed morality. Again we would express the timid hope that Christian students may have an important mission in our situation. They have less to lose not only materially but also psychologically. Not yet fulltime vassals of the kings of this world, they are more free to call them naked. They have the resources of youthful imagination that will not draw back prematurely from grappling with the possibilities of existence. It is still too early to say whether the recent stirrings of a new moral and political commitment among American students are more than straws in the wind. But Christians, more than others, should hope for more anger.

It might be appropriate, then, to close this essay with some remarks about the nature of Christian rebellion. We would argue that Christian rebellion will have two essential characteristics— its lack of principle and its lack of mythology. Saying that Christians lack principle is the same thing as saying that they have a humanistic bias. Very often, in ordinary language, the point at which people begin to talk about their principles signals some surrender of human sensitivity. They are then explaining why they have to sacrifice persons to whatever principles are supposed to be involved. Christian ethics will always ignore principles in favor of persons. It will see through the moral ambiguity of human philosophies and political positions. Its concern will always be with real, living men and women. Thus,

Christian rebellion in the South is not against the principle of segregation or for the principle of democracy. It is against oppressors and for those they oppress. Christian rebellion will always stay close to human life, human suffering, human hope. Closely related to this lack of principle is a lack of mythology. And here perhaps we can see most clearly what distinguishes Christian rebellion from most of the revolutionary movements of our time.

The work of men like Georges Sorel and Karl Mannheim has given social scientists an awareness of the importance of myth in society. What is important to see is that both "liberal" and "conservative" movements possess mythologies that often are elaborate and systematic delusions concerning the nature of social reality. "Liberals" will tend to have delusions about the future, "conservatives" about the present. Christian rebellion, which is on behalf of men and not of principles, can afford to be clear-sighted about both present and future. The Christian who seeks justice in obedience to God's will should see through the vested interests, the collective egotism, and the bad faith of the ideologies that claim "O.K.ness" of the *status quo*. He will refuse to regard the present order of society as ultimate truth and will reject the claim to that effect as an offense to God, who alone is ultimate truth. His attitude to the present order may on occasion be positive in detail, but it will always remain critical. To the extent that he maintains this critical posture, he will be detached from society, in it but not of it, always ready for an exodus in obedience to God's command. At the same time, the Christian cannot share the illusions about some future order that "liberals" so often indulge in. The Christian faith has a fairly pessimistic conception of human nature and must remain skeptical concerning projects that are based on excessive expectations as to what men are capable of. Furthermore, the Christian has his own eschatology and thus has no use for the synthetic eschatologies of modern revolutionary ideologies. He waits for the *parousia* of the risen Lord, not for a perfect society to be built in history. Christian rebellion, therefore, can never be total revolution. It rebels against injustice and untruth with passion, but its goals are limited. Its anger is tempered by compassion and humor. Even in the act of rebellion, the Christian continues to live in the wide world of God's creation. He retains his capacity for joy and for laughter. He does not mistake his own impatience for a necessity of history.

With this we have come to the end of our argument. We have nothing more to say. The continuation of the argument is in personal dialogue and in existential choice. If this essay has contributed some little light to the scene on which all of us must make our choices, then it has been worth while. The rest is not in our hands.

Notes

The intent of these notes is not to provide an exhaustive documentation. The notes are designed rather to explicate the main sources which the writer has used and to give some leads to the reader who would like to pursue further the questions discussed in the body of the text. Gerhard Lenski, *The Religious Factor* (Garden City, N.Y.: Doubleday, 1961), probably one of the best sociological studies of American religion to appear in years, came out after this essay had gone into print. Lenski's highly intriguing findings could thus not be considered in our analysis.

Chapter 1

[1] For a good discussion of this cf. the introductory material in Arnold Rose (ed.), *The Institutions of Advanced Societies* (Minneapolis: University of Minnesota Press, 1958).

[2] Daniel Lerner, *The Passing of Traditional Society* (Glencoe, Ill.: Free Press, 1958), p. 27f.

[3] Cf. Peter Drucker, *The New Society* (New York, 1950).

[4] Robert Jungk, *Brighter Than a Thousand Suns* (London: Gollancz, 1958), p. 198.

[5] Ibid., loc. cit.

[6] John Galbraith, *The Affluent Society* (Boston: Houghton Mifflin, 1958).

[7] Cf. C. B. Hoover and B. U. Ratchford, *Economic Resources and Policies of the South* (New York, 1951).

[8] Cf. Vance Packard, *The Waste Makers* (New York: David McKay, 1960).

[9] James Burnham, *The Managerial Revolution* (New York, 1941); cf. A. A. Berle and G. C. Means, *The Modern Corporation and Private Property* (New York: Macmillan, 1934).

[10] Cf. Galbraith, op. cit., p. 251ff.

[11] Cf. Population Division, U. N. Department of Social Affairs, *The Determinants and Consequences of Population Trends* (New York: United Nations, 1953); ibid., *The Future Growth of World Population* (New York: United Nations, 1958).

[12] Cf. Editors of *Fortune, The Exploding Metropolis* (Garden City, N.Y.: Doubleday, 1958).

[13] Cf. Joseph Kahl, *The American Class Structure* (New York: Rinehart, 1959); Seymour Lipset and Reinhard Bendix, *Social Mobility in Industrial Society* (Berkeley: University of California Press, 1959); Rolf Dahrendorf, *Class and Class Conflict in Industrial Society* (Stanford: Stanford University Press, 1959).

[14] Cf. Bernard Rosenberg and David White (eds.), *Mass Culture* (Glencoe, Ill.: Free Press, 1957).

[15] C. Wright Mills, *The Power Elite* (New York: Oxford University Press, 1956).

[16] Lerner, op. cit., p. 50f.

[17] William Whyte, *The Organization Man* (New York: Simon and Schuster, 1956).

[18] Cf. Ernest Dichter, *The Strategy of Desire* (Garden City, N.Y.: Doubleday, 1960).

[19] Cf. Max Lerner, *America as a Civilization* (London: Jonathan Cape, 1958), p. 666ff.

[20] Pitirim Sorokin, *The American Sex Revolution* (Boston, 1956).

[21] David Riesman, *The Lonely Crowd* (New Haven: Yale University Press, 1950). Also cf. Maurice Stein e. a. (eds.), *Identity and Anxiety* (Glencoe, Ill.: Free Press, 1960).

Chapter 2

[1] Cf. Robin Williams, *American Society* (New York: Knopf, 1954), p. 304ff; Max Lerner, *America as a Civilization* (London: Jonathan Cape, 1958), p. 701ff.

[2] Cf. Jerald Brauer, *Protestantism in America* (Philadelphia: Westminster Press, 1953); H. Richard Niebuhr, *The Kingdom of God in America* (Chicago: Willett, Clark, 1937); William Sweet, *American Culture and Religion* (Dallas: Southern Methodist University Press, 1951).

[3] Cf. Will Herberg, *Protestant—Catholic—Jew* (Garden City, N.Y.: Doubleday, 1955), p. 59ff. A. Roy Eckardt, *The Surge of Piety in America* (New York: Association Press, 1958); Martin Marty, *The New Shape of American Religion* (New York: Harper, 1959).

[4] Marty, op. cit., p. 15.

[5] Cf. the symposium on "Religion and the Intellectuals," *Partisan Review*, 1950—perhaps a classic of this new religious preoccupation among the "intelligentsia."

[6] Cf. William Miller, "Piety Along the Potomac," *The Reporter*, August 17, 1954.

[7] Marty introduces the concept of "religious establishment" into his discussion of the new situation in America (op. cit., p. 20). It seems to me, however, that the following chapters of this essay will make

clear that the concept is used here in a more radical form probably
not intended by Marty.

8 Cf. my article, "The Problem of Christian Community in Modern Society,"
Lutheran World, June 1960.

Chapter 3

1 Franklin Littell, *The German Phoenix* (Garden City, N.Y.: Doubleday,
1960), p. 170.

2 Cf. Robin Williams, *American Society* (New York: Knopf, 1954), p. 372 ff.

3 Cf. ibid., p. 388ff.

4 Robert and Helen Lynd, *Middletown in Transition* (New York: Harcourt,
Brace, 1937), p. 402ff.

5 Ibid., p. 316.

6 Ibid., p. 317.

7 Will Herberg, *Protestant—Catholic—Jew* (Garden City, N.Y.: Doubleday, 1955), p. 102ff.

8 Martin Marty, *The New Shape of American Religion* (New York: Harper,
1959), p. 31ff.

9 Herberg, loc. cit.

10 Max Weber, *The Protestant Ethic and the Spirit of Capitalism* (London:
George Allen & Unwin, 1930).

11 I am indebted for this story to Benton Johnson, University of Oregon.

12 Cf. Hans Gerth and C. Wright Mills, *Character and Social Structure*
(New York, 1953).

13 This point was made by Eugen Rosenstock-Huessy in a comparison between Confucius and John Dewey: *The Christian Future* (New
York: Scribner's, 1946), p. 42ff.

14 Cf. my article on American funeral customs in *Koelner Zeitschrift fuer
Sozilogie und Sozialpsychologie,* 1960, 12:2 (with R. Lieban).

15 William Whyte, *The Organization Man* (New York: Simon & Schuster,
1956).

16 In courses taught at the New School for Social Research. The picture of
the "central core," flanked on the "left" by the sects and on the
"right" by the liturgical churches, is also taken from Mayer.

17 Robert Lee, *The Social Sources of Church Unity* (New York: Abingdon,
1960), p. 187ff.

18 Cf. Emile Durkheim, *The Elementary Forms of the Religious Life*
(Glencoe, Ill.: Free Press, 1947).

19 Cf. Bronislaw Malinowski, *The Foundations of Faith and Morals* (Lon-
don: Oxford University Press, 1936); ibid., *A Scientific Theory
of Culture* (Chapel Hill: University of North Carolina Press, 1944);
William Goode, *Religion Among the Primitives* (Glencoe, Ill.: Free
Press, 1951); J. Milton Yinger, *Religion, Society and the Individual*
(New York: Macmillan, 1957).

[20] Yinger, op. cit., p. 71.

[21] Talcott Parsons, *Structure and Process in Modern Societies* (Glencoe, Ill.: Free Press, 1960), p. 315.

[22] W. Lloyd Warner, *The Living and the Dead* (New Haven: Yale University Press, 1959), p. 277.

[23] Cf. ibid., p. 255ff.

[24] Arthur Vidich and Joseph Bensman, *Small Town in Mass Society* (Princeton: Princeton University Press, 1958), esp. part IV.

[25] Ibid., p. 258.

[26] Ibid. p. 304ff.

[27] A. C. Spectorsky, *The Exurbanites* (New York: Berkley Publishing Corp., 1958).

[28] John Seeley e. a., *Crestwood Heights* (New York: Basic Books, 1956).

[29] Maurice Stein, *The Eclipse of Community* (Princeton: Princeton University Press, 1960), p. 293f.

Chapter 4

[1] A classic work on the subject is Anson Stokes, *Church and State in the United States* (New York: Harper, 1950). For a briefer study cf. Leo Pfeffer, *Church, State and Freedom* (Boston: Beacon Press, 1953).

[2] In this discussion of the relationship between religion and the state I am once more heavily indebted to the teaching of Carl Mayer at the New School for Social Research.

[3] Daniel Boorstin, *The Genius of American Politics* (Chicago: University of Chicago Press, 1953), p. 133ff.

[4] In addition to the work of Boorstin just quoted, cf. Will Herberg, *Protestant—Catholic—Jew* (Garden City, N.Y.: Doubleday, 1955), p. 85ff; Martin Marty, *The New Shape of American Religion* (New York: Harper, 1959), p. 67ff; Reinhold Niebuhr, *The Irony of American History* (New York: Scribner's, 1952).

[5] Quoted in Herberg, op. cit., p. 97.

[6] Quoted in Boorstin, op. cit., p. 146.

[7] Quoted in Marty, op. cit., p. 83.

[8] Ibid., loc. cit.

[9] Cf. Pfeffer, op. cit., *passim*.

[10] Quoted in ibid., p. 157. The dissenting opinions of Justices Black and Jackson express a spirited attack on the permissive conception of separation embodied in the majority decision.

[11] Cf. the analysis of this in Theodore Powell, *The School Bus Law* (Middletown, Conn.: Wesleyan University Press, 1960).

[12] Quoted in ibid., p. 18.

[13] Quoted in Herberg, op. cit., p. 102.

[14] Waldo Burchard, "Role Conflicts of Military Chaplains," in J. Milton Yinger, *Religion, Society and the Individual* (New York: Macmillan, 1957), p. 586ff.

[15] Ibid., p. 595f.

[16] Boorstin, op. cit., p. 135.

[17] Kenneth Underwood, *Protestant and Catholic* (Boston: Beacon Press, 1957), p. 303.

Chapter 5

[1] Cf. H. H. Gerth and C. W. Mills (eds.), *From Max Weber* (New York: Oxford University Press, 1958), p. 302ff.

[2] Cf. Robin Williams, *American Society* (New York: Knopf, 1954), p. 78ff; also cf. the references given in footnote 13 for chapter 1.

[3] Max Lerner, *America as a Civilization* (London: Jonathan Cape, 1958), p. 525.

[4] Robert Lee, *The Social Sources of Church Unity* (New York: Abingdon, 1960), p. 104f.

[5] H. Richard Niebuhr, *The Social Sources of Denominationalism* (New York: Henry Holt, 1929).

[6] Cf. W. L. Warner and P. S. Lunt, *The Social Life of a Modern Community* (New Haven: Yale University Press, 1941), and the subsequent volumes of the "Yankee City" series by Warner and his colleagues.

[7] Liston Pope, *Millhands and Preachers* (New Haven: Yale University Press, 1942).

[8] Ibid., p. 70.

[9] Ibid., p. 274.

[10] John Morland, *Millways of Kent* (Chapel Hill: University of North Carolina Press, 1958).

[11] Ibid., p. 110.

[12] James West, *Plainville, U.S.A.* (New York: Columbia University Press, 1945).

[13] Ibid., p. 143.

[14] Arthur Vidich and Joseph Bensman, *Small Town in Mass Society* (Princeton: Princeton University Press, 1958), p. 251f.

[15] Kenneth Underwood, *Protestant and Catholic* (Boston: Beacon Press, 1957).

[16] Ibid., p. 189.

[17] Frederick Shippey, "The City Church and Social Class," pamphlet published by Methodist Division of National Missions, Philadelphia, 1958, p. 18.

[18] Ibid., loc. cit.

[19] Cf., for instance, John Holt, "Holiness Religion," *American Sociological Review*, October 1940, or the material on Negro religion in Hylan Lewis, *Blackways of Kent* (Chapel Hill: University of North Carolina Press, 1955).

[20] Benton Johnson, "A Critical Appraisal of the Church-Sect Typology," *American Sociological Review,* February 1957.

[21] Ibid., p. 92.

[22] Cf., for instance, C. Y. Glock and B. B. Ringer, "Church Policy and the Attitudes of Ministers and Parishioners on Social Issues," *American Sociological Review,* April 1956.

[23] Ernest Campbell and Thomas Pettigrew, *Christians in Racial Crisis* (Washington: Public Affairs Press, 1959), p. 122ff.

Chapter 6

[1] Cf. William Miller, "The Gospel of Norman Vincent Peale," *Union Seminary Quarterly Review,* January 1955.

[2] For a summary of various theories in the psychology of religion, cf. Michael Argyle, *Religious Behaviour* (London: Routledge & Kegan Paul, 1958), p. 140ff; also cf. J. Milton Yinger, *Religion, Society and the Individual* (New York: Macmillan, 1957), p. 73ff.

[3] Robert and Helen Lynd, *Middletown* (New York: Harcourt, Brace, 1956—the original publication was in 1929), p. 366f.

[4] Ibid., p. 369.

[5] Ibid., p. 370.

[6] William Whyte, *The Organization Man* (Doubleday soft-cover edition), p. 406f.

[7] Ibid., p. 418.

[8] Cf. especially John Seeley e. a., *Crestwood Heights* (New York: Basic Books, 1956), *passim.*

[9] Herbert Gans, "The Origin and Growth of a Jewish Community in the Suburbs," in Marshall Sklare, *The Jews* (Glencoe, Ill.: Free Press, 1958), p. 205ff.

[10] Ibid., p. 215ff.

[11] Cf. Benton Johnson, "The Development of Pastoral Counseling Programs in Protestantism," *Pacific Sociological Review,* Fall 1958.

[12] Wayne Oates, "The Cult of Reassurance," *Religion in Life,* Winter 1954.

[13] A. Roy Eckardt, *The Surge of Piety in America* (New York: Association Press, 1958), p. 57.

[14] Dan Wakefield, "Slick-Paper Christianity," in Maurice Stein e. a. (eds.), *Identity and Anxiety* (Glencoe, Ill.: Free Press, 1960), p. 414f.

[15] Frederick Elkin, "God, Radio and the Movies," in Bernard Rosenberg and David White (eds.), *Mass Culture* (Glencoe, Ill.: Free Press, 1957), p. 308ff.

[16] Ibid., p. 310.

[17] Cf., for example, James West, *Plainville, U.S.A.* (New York: Columbia University Press, 1945), p. 142ff., or John Morland, *Millways of Kent* (Chapel Hill: University of North Carolina Press, 1958), p. 105ff.

[18] Cf. Allan Eister, *Drawing Room Conversion* (Durham, N.C.: Duke University Press, 1950).

[19] Kurt and Gladys Lang, "Decisions for Christ," in Stein, op. cit., p. 427.

[20] Cf. T. W. Adorno e. a., *The Authoritarian Personality* (New York: Harper, 1950), esp. p. 208ff. and p. 727ff; Gordon Allport, *The Nature of Prejudice* (Cambridge, Mass.: Addison-Wesley, 1954), p. 444ff.

[21] Adorno, op. cit., p. 732f.

[22] Allport, op. cit., p. 454.

[23] Cf. Argyle, op. cit., p. 83ff.

[24] Rose Goldsen e. a., *What College Students Think* (Princeton: Van Nostrand, 1960), esp. cc. 7–8.

[25] Ibid., pp. 177, 179, 182, 188.

[26] Ibid., p. 178.

[27] Cf. Peter L. Berger, *The Precarious Vision—A Sociologist Looks at Social Fictions and Christian Faith* (Garden City, N.Y.: Doubleday, 1961).

Interlude

[1] Robert Miller, *American Protestantism and Social Issues, 1919–1939* (Chapel Hill: University of North Carolina Press, 1958), p. 350.

Chapter 7

[1] William Whyte, *The Organization Man* (Garden City, N.Y.: Doubleday, 1957), p. 411.

[2] Cf. Peter L. Berger, *The Precarious Vision—A Sociologist Looks at Social Fictions and Christian Faith* (Garden City, N.Y.: Doubleday, 1961).

Chapter 8

[1] Cf. my article, "The Problem of Christian Community in Modern Society," *The Lutheran World*, June 1960.

[2] Amos 5:18–24.

[3] Quoted in Franklin Littell, *The German Phoenix* (Garden City, N.Y.: Doubleday, 1960), p. 186ff.

[4] Karl Barth and Johannes Hammel, *How to Serve God in a Marxist Land* (New York: Association Press, 1959), p. 64f.

Chapter 9

[1] For a detailed discussion of the latter topic, cf. the three volumes of E. Theodore Bachmann (ed.), *Churches and Social Welfare* (New York: National Council of the Churches of Christ, 1955).

[2] The discussion of this illustration has been influenced by the example of experiments in diaconal service in Protestant churches in the Netherlands and other west-European countries.

[3] For a discussion of the development of thinking on these matters in American Protestantism, cf. Donald Meyer, *The Protestant Search for Political Realism* (Berkeley: University of California Press, 1960).

[4] Cf., for instance, the place of the churches in the decision-making processes in Floyd Hunter, *Community Power Structure* (Chapel Hill: University of North Carolina Press, 1953).

[5] For a discussion of the relationship of the Little Brothers to other innovating movements in French Catholicism, especially the worker-priests, cf. Adrien Dansette, *Destin du catholicisme français* (Paris: Flammarion, 1957).

[6] Ibid., p. 214.

[7] For a concise statement of the purposes and activities of the "Academy movement," cf. Margaret Frakes, *Bridges to Understanding* (Philadelphia: Muhlenberg Press, 1960).

[8] This example is not based on any actual project. But the procedure described is commonly used in the European laymen's institutes and has been successfully adapted in America.

[9] The Institute of Church and Community, of which the writer of this essay is director, began its "Academy" program two years ago. Since then, it has carried on conferences and discussion groups with advertisers, labor officials, personnel managers, lawyers, engineers, artists, and various interests involved in the problem of medical economics. As far as possible, seminary students are involved in these ventures, never as spectators, but in various capacities helpful to the program. Within the Hartford Seminary curriculum, insights gained in these "extramural" undertakings are communicated to students in various courses and seminars. Also, the Institute of Church and Community carries on a co-operative program with the University of Connecticut to train professional sociologists to serve the churches in teaching, research, and various forms of social engagement.

[10] Cf. Peter L. Berger, *The Precarious Vision—A Sociologist Looks at Social Fictions and Christian Faith* (Garden City, N.Y.: Doubleday, 1961), especially Part III.

Chapter 10

[1] Cf., for example, Tom Allan, *The Face of My Parish* (New York: Harper, 1953); Abbé Michonneau, *Revolution in a City Parish* (Westminster: Newman Press, 1949); Ernest Southcott, *The Parish Comes Alive* (New York: Morehouse–Gorham, 1956).

[2] Martin Marty, *The New Shape of American Religion* (New York: Harper, 1959), p. 122. Italics are Marty's.

[3] George Webber, *God's Colony in Man's World* (New York: Abingdon Press, 1960).

[4] Robert Spike, *Safe in Bondage* (New York: Friendship Press, 1960).

[5] Cf. F. E. Johnson and J. E. Ackerman, *The Church as Employer, Money Raiser, and Investor* (New York: Harper, 1959); David Holt, *Handbook of Church Finance* (New York: Macmillan, 1960).

[6] News item in the Hartford *Times,* December 13, 1960. The minimum with which a new congregation has to figure today in terms of a building campaign for a conventional church edifice is about $125,000.

[7] For an excellent study of the American Baptist Convention under this aspect, cf. Paul Harrison, *Authority and Power in the Free Church Tradition* (Princeton: Princeton University Press, 1959).

[8] At a consultation on new approaches to the laity at Parishfield in Brighton, Mich., February 1960.